FRETBOARD THEORY: FOR BEGINNERS

3 Manuscripts in 1 Book, Including: Music Theory, How to Play Guitar and How to Play Ukulele

Preston Hoffman

Table of Contents

MUSIC THEORY
FOR BEGINNERS
The Only 7 Exercises You Need to Learn
Music Fundamentals and the Elements
of Written Music Today
PRESTON HOFFMAN

BOOK 1

MUSIC THEORY: FOR BEGINNERS

The Only 7 Exercises You Need to Learn Music Fundamentals and the Elements of Written Music Today

Preston Hoffman

Table of Contents

Introduction

Thank you and congratulations on purchasing this book, *"Music Theory: For Beginners"* I have written this book to provide you with the steps that you need to take to understand the fundamentals of music theory from a beginner's standpoint.

One of the most common problems that many people face when it comes to music theory is the inability to get a good book that sticks to the fundamental aspects. Music theory is not exactly a topic that will get your heart pounding, so most people want content that will explain music fundamentals in a clear and concise manner. Most music theory books either bore the reader with long, drawn-out explanations, or they toss in some complex concepts that leave you totally confused.

However, this is where this book is different. This book provides you with the only seven exercises that you need as a beginner to master the fundamental elements of written music. These interactive exercises are all based on seven topics that form the basis of every good music theory course. The exercises are spread throughout the book so that once you finish reading each chapter, you can test yourself. I have taken the time to make the questions as challenging as possible yet simple enough for any beginner to understand. In any case, the answers have been provided at the end of the book.

You will not find yourself struggling with complex theories here. I have written this book with the beginner in mind, so every chapter covers a single aspect of music theory. This is to ensure that you move step-by-step, mastering one foundational topic before you move onto the next one. You will learn the common notation system, scales, clefs, key signatures, intervals, chords, and much more.

I have tried to make sure that the topics move sequentially in terms of the level of difficulty. My goal is to take your hand and walk you through every topic and exercise so that you feel comfortable with the content. From my experience with reading and writing music, I know that if you get the first step right, then the next one will automatically fall into place.

By the time you finish reading this book, you will be much more confident in reading and even writing your own music. Yes, it's true! The exercises you will go through in this book will test you and help you grow your musical abilities. I can promise you that with this book, you will finally get to learn all you ever wanted to know about music theory in a fun and interactive way. This is a personal guarantee!

Are you ready? Let's go!

Chapter One: Understanding Music Theory

In this chapter, you will learn about what music theory is all about and why it is important for beginners to have a firm theoretical foundation. You will also go through a brief and painless history of written music. Finally, you will get to discover the seven exercises that are fundamental to the learning of music.

What is Music Theory?

The simplest way to define music theory is this: It is the language that enables you to read, understand, and play any kind of music that has been composed. Music theory is made up of rules and concepts that are designed to govern the way music is written and performed.

Another way to look at it is that music is a language that consists of many various parts. Each part is then divided into smaller sections. If you want to learn how to speak the whole language, you must start by learning the smaller sections first and how to combine them to form the larger parts. Then you must learn how to put together those large parts to communicate whatever message you have through that language.

We learn music theory so that we know how to put the elements together to compose music. That is music theory in a nutshell.

As a beginner, it is easy to fall into the trap of feeling overwhelmed when you hear the words "music theory," but there is really nothing to worry about. The critical thing to keep in mind when learning about music theory is that the music preceded the theory. The art of making musical sounds dates back thousands of years, and at that time, our ancestors didn't have any kind of theory to rely on. They just pounded on their drums and played it by ear. If you are already playing an instrument, then you most likely have a rough idea about music theory. The only issue is that you haven't learned the terms and technicalities yet.

Like I said before, music theory is a language that allows musicians to read and perform compositions the way the composer intended. However, it is important to also note that there are some musicians who are not able to read or write music, yet they can still make awesome melodies and sounds. There are some people who can hear and speak English but cannot read or write it. Therefore, some people view learning music theory as boring and unnecessary.

On the other hand, I believe that a student can progress much further in learning a new language by training himself/herself to read and write it. It is the same with music theory. If you want to master new techniques, gain more confidence, and perform new styles, you need to learn music theory.

Now let's go back a bit into history to unearth the beginnings of music theory.

Musical Beginnings

According to historians, complex musical instruments were already being used as far back as 7000 B.C. Archaeologists have found bone flutes that can still be used to create short performances for modern listeners to hear.

There are pictographs from 3500 B.C. that depict the ancient Egyptians playing clarinets, harps, and lyres. By the year 1500 B.C., the people in Northern Syria had modified the Egyptian harp and created the first ever two-stringed guitar. The instrument even had tuning pegs and a hollow soundboard for amplifying sounds.

So why am I telling you all this?

If you look at the history of ancient music, you will realize that distinct cultures spread out all over the world were able to create music with very similar tonal qualities. How was this possible? It is believed that certain patterns of musical notes just sound right while others do not. If this is the case, then music theory is simply the search for why and how certain notes sound right or wrong. To put it more plainly, music theory is important because it helps us understand *why* an object sounds a particular way and *how* we can reproduce that exact sound.

Ancient Greece is believed to be the origin of music theory. The Greeks even built schools that taught the science and philosophy of analysing music. It was Pythagoras who went as far as creating the 12-pitch octave scale that resembles the one we currently use today. Pythagoras achieved this using a device known as the Circle of Fifths, which you will learn about later in this book.

A lot of the musical theory you are about to learn is based on the works of the ancient Greeks. But unlike the Greek language, this book is much simpler to read and understand.

The Significance of Theory in Your Music

It is easy to think that making great music is as simple as sitting down, playing whatever note you want, going in any direction you see fit, and even stopping at any stage of the performance. That is often the view of most aspiring musicians who would love to play an instrument.

However, such kind of performances, if they do exist, would cause confusion and sound annoying to the listeners. Only those musicians who have thoroughly mastered how to stack notes and chords adjacent to each other can manage to perform a spontaneous jam that listeners would love. In other words, since music is a language that communicates a message, you must learn how to connect with your listeners at all times.

Learning musical theory can also inspire you a great deal, as you will soon find out after you finish reading this book. It is a tremendously great feeling when you discover that you can put together a chord progression and create an awesome song out of it. How would you feel if you could look at a piece of classical music and know that you can play it for the first time?

What about being confident enough to call up your friends and ask them to come over and jam with you? You wouldn't be able to do that without learning music theory since you need a way to communicate with other musicians. You use music theory to talk to one another as you play your various instruments.

The truth is that music theory will broaden your horizons as a musician. If you see yourself as a potential rock guitarist, you will be able to know which notes to play in which key. If it's classical music you are interested in, you will know how to sight-read and maintain a consistent beat. Music is fun but it also requires a prominent level of discipline. At the end of it all, it is worth it!

The Seven Fundamental Exercises

There are a lot of elements that you will have to learn to become an accomplished musician. Of course, we all wish that we could somehow sit down with an instrument and start playing beautiful music without going through the hassle of any formal training. But the reality is that you need structured exercises that will prepare you for your future as a music maestro.

In the next few chapters, we are going to cover music theory fundamentals that will help you get started. There are seven elements that you will have to master to learn these elements effectively. They are:

1. Learning the staff and music alphabet

2. Common notation

3. Basic elements of music (rhythm, melody, harmony, etc)

4. Mastering the scales

5. Building intervals

6. Understanding key signatures

7. Forming chords

Every single one of these elements is critical to your progress as a beginner. They will teach you the individual elements of music and how they are put together to create a solid foundation for reading, playing, and studying music.

Chapter Summary

Here is a summary of the key points of this chapter:

- Music theory is the rules and concepts that enable us to read, understand, and play any kind of musical composition.
- It is possible to play music without learning music theory, but if you want to go further in learning new techniques and performing new styles, you must learn music theory.
- Though complex musical instruments date back as far as 7000 B.C., the ancient Greeks are the ones credited with establishing schools for analysing the elements of music.
- Learning musical theory will enable you to communicate more effectively with listeners and fellow musicians, while also inspiring confidence in your own musical abilities.
- There are seven key exercises that will help you learn the fundamentals of music theory.

In the next chapter, you will learn about the staff and how we use the music alphabet to write music. It isn't a difficult topic, but since the rest of the book will be based on what you learn in the next chapter, you need to make sure that you go through it thoroughly.

Chapter Two: Learning the Staff

In this chapter, you will learn about the staff. It is important to start by learning the main way that we write music. You will learn what the staff looks like, the several types of clefs, and how to arrange notes when writing your music. There will also an exercise at the end of the chapter to test what you have learned.

Human beings started making music way before writing was invented. Even to this day, some musicians choose to play "by ear," which means they don't rely on written music. However, it is important to write music so that it can be shared and studied. This means that we must have system to represent music, hence the need for a music alphabet.

What is the Music Alphabet?

The musical alphabet is an arrangement of letters that enables us to write the sounds that we want to play. Every time you sit down to play music with others, the first thing you do is talk about what you plan on playing. By talking I don't mean just telling each other stories or describing your music verbally. The language of communication should be specific to music, and that is where the music alphabet comes in. The alphabet is the means of representing your music.

Before we go into the musical notes themselves, let's start by learning about the most widespread way of writing music. This is the staff.

The Staff

Now that you have learned about the music alphabet, it's time to tackle a very important component of music. All instruments that play specific pitches are written on the staff, which is comprised of five horizontal parallel lines. Music notes are usually placed either on the lines or in the spaces between the lines. The music on a staff is read from left to right.

In the image below, you will notice some short lines that are above or below the staff. These are known as *ledger lines*. These are used to show a note that is too low or too high to be placed on the staff.

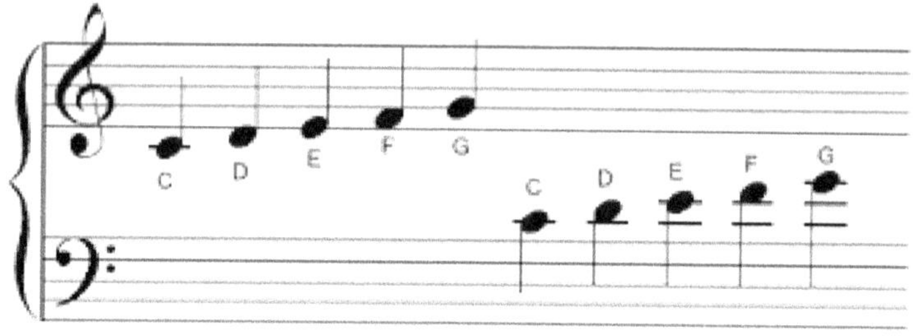

Figure 2.1

To make reading music much easier, vertical lines are used to split the staff into sections. These lines are known as ***bar lines***. Each section that is formed on the staff is then called a ***measure*** or ***bar***. At the end of every staff, there are two lines that mark the end of a section of music or song. These are known as ***double bar lines***. A heavy double bar line indicates that you have reached the end of the song. A light double bar line means the end of a section of music.

Figure 2.2

You may be wondering what some of the symbols and shapes are on the staff above. These will be discussed later in this chapter.

Clefs

In figure 2.2, you notice a symbol that is placed at the beginning of the staff. This is the ***Clef symbol***. It tells you the type of note that is found on every line and space of the staff. There are two kinds of clefs; the treble clef (or G clef) and the bass clef (or F clef).

The reason why it's called a G clef is that its body curls around the line that represents the G note. For the F clef, the symbol curls around the line representing the F note. The notes in the staff are always arranged in ascending order from top to bottom, but they are positioned differently depending on the type of clef being used. The reason why we use different clefs is to cover as many notes within the human voice range as possible, as well as most of the instruments used. People and instruments with high voice ranges use the treble clef while those with lower ranges use bass clef.

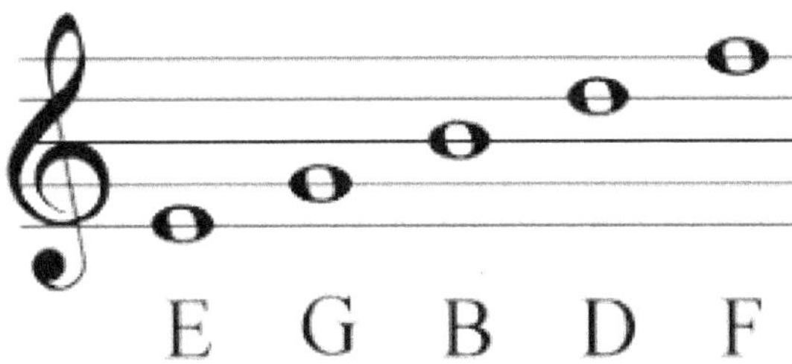

Figure 2.3

Figure 2.4

Exercise 1

1. Draw the staff on a piece of paper and practice writing the two clef symbols on the staff. Draw as many as you can until you learn it perfectly.

2. Draw the staff with treble and name all the spaces on the staff.

3. Draw the staff with bass clef and name the lines in it.

4. On a staff with a treble clef, name the ledger lines and spaces above the staff.

5. On a staff with a bass clef, name the lines and spaces below the staff.

Chapter Summary

Here are some key points you need to remember:

- The musical alphabet is an arrangement of letters that enable us to write the sounds that we want to play.
- The notes on the staff are placed either on the lines or in the spaces between the lines.
- Notes on the staff are arranged in ascending order.
- Ledger lines are used when showing notes that are too high or too low to appear on the staff.
- A bar line splits the staff into sections called measures or bars.
- A heavy double bar line indicates the end of a song.
- A light double bar line indicates the end of a section of music.
- There are two types of clef symbols – the treble clef and the bass clef.

In the next chapter, you will learn about music notation. These are considered the building blocks of music and are necessary when writing your music.

Chapter Three: Understanding Common Notation

In this chapter, you will learn the A-B-C's of the musical language. We will talk about the building blocks that form the foundation of musical theory. These include notes, pitch, octave, beats, and time signature. There will also an exercise at the end of the chapter to test what you have learned.

Common notation simply refers to the standard system that we use to represent music notes. It is more widely used than other types of music notation that have been invented, for example, tablature. You have already learned about one part of common notation in the previous chapter. Now let's talk about notes and pitches.

Notes

Every piece of music you will encounter consists of notes. They are the building blocks of music. A note is simply a letter of the musical alphabet that represents the *pitch* made by a musical instrument.

The pitch of a note refers to how low or high it sounds. Pitch is dependent on the frequency and wavelength of the sound wave of a note. If the frequency of the sound wave is high, and the wavelength is short, the pitch will be high. Since very few musicians are keen on such kind of physics terminologies, they use letters to represent different pitches.

There are seven letters that form the music alphabet. These are:

A B C D E F G A

or:

C D E F G A B C

These seven letters are used to name the white keys on a keyboard. As you can see above, you start with the letter A and proceed to the letter G. After G, instead of going to H, we go back and start counting from A. In music, each set of seven letters (A – G or C - B) is referred to as an ***octave***. The moment you reach the eighth note, you begin the next octave.

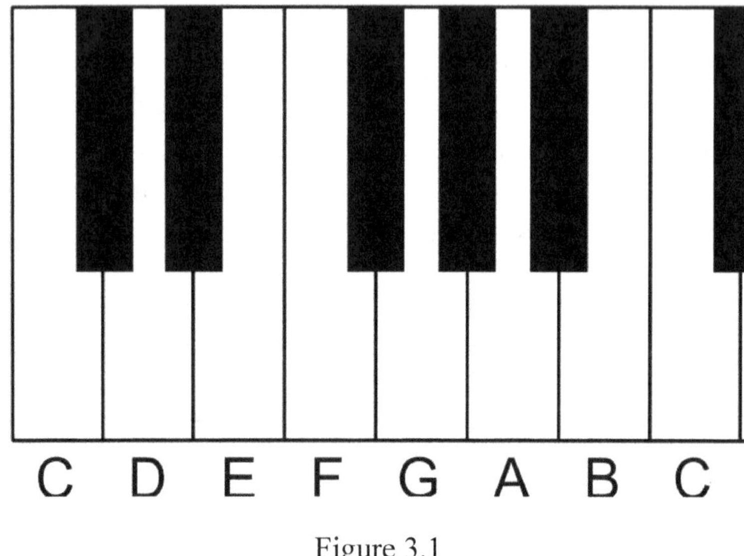

Figure 3.1

But there's one thing that you need to be keenly aware of here. As you move toward the right side, or *up the alphabet*, you realize that you will meet a note with the same letter name as another one before. However, this next note will be at a higher octave than the previous one.

In figure 3.1 above, the second C note has a pitch that is at a higher octave than the first. If you were to move up the alphabet, the third C note would be a higher pitch than the second one, and so on. You can also move in the opposite direction, and this is referred to as going *down the alphabet*.

Sharps and Flats

Though there are only seven letters in the music alphabet, there are more than seven notes. The seven letters from A to G represent *natural* notes. Natural simply means it is a regular note. However, there are five other notes that are usually placed in-between these natural notes. This brings the total number of notes in the music alphabet to 12. These five other notes are represented as *sharp notes* (♯) and *flat notes* (♭).

A sharp note is a note that is higher in pitch than its natural letter. For example, G♯ (pronounced G sharp) is higher than G. On the other hand, a flat note is a note lower than its natural letter, so A♭ (pronounced A flat) is lower in pitch than A. These sharp and flat notes are used to represent the black keys on a keyboard.

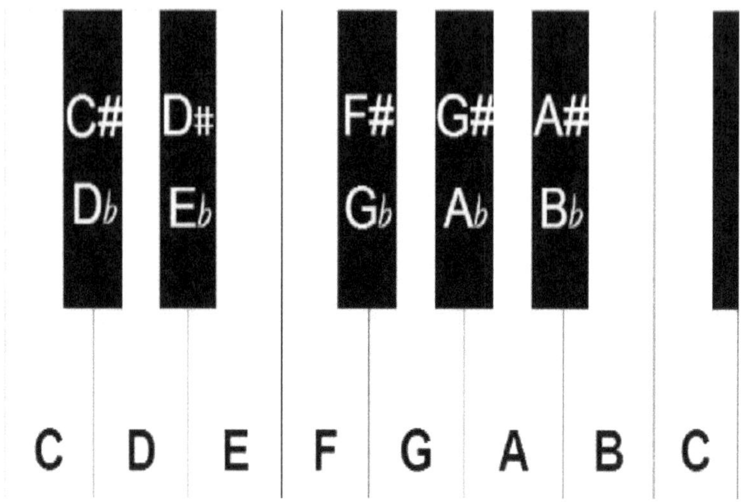

Figure 3.2

From the image above, you can see that in some instances, the sharps and flats occupy the same key. This means that they refer to the same note but are given different names depending on where they are used. This is what is known as ***enharmonics***. In other words, F♯ is the same note as G♭, and C♯ is the same note as D♭, and so on.

If you are keen, you may have noticed that there are some notes that do not have any sharps or flats between them. This happens between the E-F notes and B-C notes. This shouldn't be taken to mean that there is no E♯ or C♭. We simply refer to them as F or B. So, when you raise an E by one note you get an F. Also, when you lower a C note you get a B.

The sharp symbol usually indicates that the particular note is one half-step higher than its natural equivalent. For example, G♯ is one half-step higher than G. In the same way, the flat symbol indicates that the note is one half-step lower than its natural equivalent. So, A♭ is one half-step lower than A.

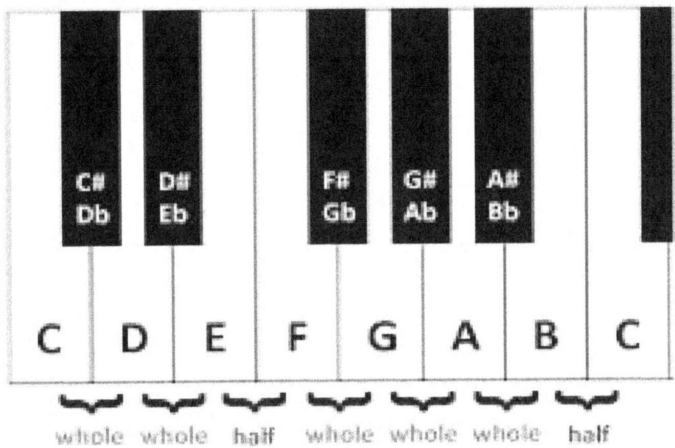

Figure 3.3

In other words, the distance between the G note and the A note is *one whole step*. When you see two adjacent notes having a sharp or a flat note between them, then that means that they are a whole step apart. Therefore, from figure 3.3, it is clear to see that most of the notes on the keyboard are one whole step apart except the E-F notes and B-C notes. These are only one half-step apart.

Parts of a Note

In common notation, sounds are written in form of notes. The two most critical pieces of information that written music should convey to a musician are the pitch to be played and its duration. A note that is placed high on the staff should be played at a higher sound.

To determine the pitch of a note, look at the clef, key signature, and the line or space the note is placed. To determine the duration of a note (how long it lasts), you look at the shape of the note, its tempo, and time signature.

There are three specific parts of a note. There is the head, the stem, and the flag.

- **The Head** (3) – This is the rounded section of a note. The head can be shaded or hollow. Every note must have a head.

- **The Stem** (2) – This is the vertical straight line that is linked to the head. Quavers, crotchets and minims all contain stems. Stems can point either up or down depending on the position of the note on the staff. Notes on or above the centre line have stems pointing down. Notes below the centre line have stems pointing up.

- **The Flag** (1) – This is the line that sticks out from the top or bottom of the stem. Only quavers and shorter notes carry flags.

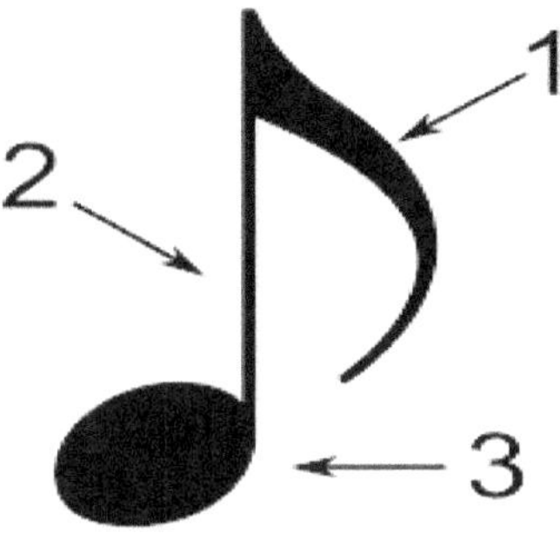

Figure 3.4

The pitch of a note is determined by the position of the head of the note, not the entire body. The head, the stem and the flag are all factors that must be considered when deciding how much time a note is given.

Note Duration and Values

Note duration is defined as the amount of time that a note is played. Each note usually has its own value, and these include the semibreve, minim, crotchet, quaver, and semiquaver. They are shown in this exact order in the image below.

Figure 3.5

The Whole (Semibreve) Note

This note is represented by a hollow oval and has no stem. It is the longest note in modern music and lasts for a full four beats.

This means that for four entire beats, all you must do is play and hold that one note.

The Half (Minim) Note

This is half the value of a semibreve and is held for half as long as the whole note. Two minims occupy the same length of time as a semibreve. It is represented by a hollow oval with a stem.

The Quarter (Crotchet) Note

This is a quarter of a semibreve. Four crotchets occupy the same length of time as a semibreve, which means a crotchet is one beat long. It is represented by a shaded oval with a stem.

The Eighth (Quaver) Note

This is half the length of time as a crotchet. It is represented by a shaded oval with a stem and a flag. The flag cuts the value of a note by half.

The Sixteenth (Semiquaver) Note

Two semiquavers occupy the same length of time as one quaver. It is represented by a shaded oval with a stem and two flags.

If two notes that have flags are next to each other, they are sometimes connected using a *beam*. This makes it possible to group flagged notes so that the music is easier and faster to read. The same principle also applies to semiquavers. A note must have the same number of beams as it does flags.

Figure 3.6: Semiquaver with beam

Dotted Notes

By now you know that a minim is half the length of a semibreve; a crotchet is half of a minim, and so on. But what do you do if you want a note length that is not half of another note? That's where the dotted note comes in. A dotted note is 1 ½ times the length of the same note. So, you end up with the original note length and half of that note length. For example, a dotted minim would have a duration that is as long as a minim plus a crotchet; or three crotchets.

If a note has two dots, it simply means that each dot adds half the length of the previous note. This is shown in figure 3.7 below.

Figure 3.7

Time Signatures

These are usually indicated at the front end of the staff and are placed after the clef symbol and key signature. The time signature doesn't appear on every staff. It is used only when there is a change in the meter. ***Meter*** refers to the basic rhythm of the music. Time signature represents the meter and tells you how you should write it.

A fraction represents time signatures. The number at the top indicates the number of beats per measure while the number at the bottom indicates the type of note that will be used to carry the beat. The next section explains this more clearly.

Figure 3.7

Beats

There are many ways to organize music, and one of them is by splitting the time into small periods known as ***beats***. Most of the actions that go with a piece of music occur at the start of the beat. For example, when you tap your foot or clap your hands, you are making those sounds or movements at the start of the beat. This is usually referred to as being "on the downbeat" since it corresponds to the moment when the conductor's baton reaches the bottom of its path.

The downbeat is the most substantial section of a beat, though some are stronger than the rest. Beats form a pattern such as strong-weak-weak-strong-weak-weak. Therefore, beats are further grouped into measures or bars. For example, a beat such as strong-weak-weak-strong-weak-weak would be written as 1-2-3-1-2-3, which means that each measure must contain three beats.

We already talked about how time signature indicates the number of beats per measure and the kind of note that carries a beat. For example, figure 3.7 has a time signature that requires three quarter (crotchet) notes in all the measures on that particular staff. In other words, every measure will have three crotchets. We usually say that such a piece is in "three four" time.

Don't forget what we learned earlier. A crotchet (quarter) note is one beat long. In other words, every measure on the staff should have the equivalent of three beats. These can still be represented as one minim and a crotchet, or six quavers per measure.

Exercise 2

1. Complete the following series of natural notes: A B
   _ _ E F _ _

2. Provide an alternative name for the following:

   a. A♯

   b. D♭

   c. G♭

   d. E♭

Fill in the blanks:

3. 1 semibreve = ____________ quavers

4. 1 minim = ____________ quarters

5. 1 minim = 1 quarter + __________ eighths

6. Draw two staves with a treble clef symbol and time signatures showing *two four-time*, *three eight time*, and *six four time*. Fill in each measure with a different combination of note lengths. Use at least one dotted note in each staff.

Chapter Summary

Here are some of the key points you need to remember:

- A note is a letter that represents the pitch made by a musical instrument.
- An octave is a set of notes from one letter to the next pitch by the same letter name.
- The symbol ♯ represents sharp notes.
- Flat notes are represented by the symbol♭.
- Enharmonics are two notes that have equal pitches but are known by different names.
- There are five note values - semibreve, minim, quarter, quaver, and semiquaver. Each note lasts half the beat of the previous one.
- Music is divided into short time periods called beats.
- The time signature is shown using a fraction. The number at the top indicates the number of beats per measure. The number at the bottom indicates the type of note that will be used to carry the beat.

In the next chapter, you will learn about the building blocks of music. These are the basic elements of every musical piece, and they include aspects like rhythm, harmony, melody, timbre, and dynamics.

Chapter Four: The Basic Elements Music

In this chapter, you will learn about the essential elements that make music what it really is. These are aspects that even non-musicians can understand. As long as you have an appreciation for good music, you should be able to pick out these musical building blocks.

We are going to cover a number of these basic elements here. It is also important to note that musical theory experts hold differing opinions as to the total number of the elements of music. Some claim that there are as few as four while others say that there are as many as 10. Here we shall be covering rhythm, harmony, melody, timbre, texture, and dynamics.

Creating Rhythm

The primary reason why we study music theory is to be able to describe different musical pieces regarding how similar or different they are about the above six elements. Rhythm is considered one of the most basic components of any kind of music. Some types of music don't have harmony or melody, but every piece of music must have rhythm.

So, what exactly is rhythm?

Rhythm can be defined as the pattern of sounds repeated throughout the music. We can also say that rhythm is the arrangement of note lengths in music. Music and time go hand in hand, which means that rhythm has to be heard over a period of time. Rhythm is usually shaped by the meter and incorporates other elements such as *tempo* and *beat*.

Tempo is the speed at which you play a particular piece of music. When creating a composition, you indicate the tempo using an Italian word. For example, if you look at the starting point of a score, you may see words like *Largo* (slow pace), *Moderato* (moderate pace), or *Presto* (very fast pace). Here are some common tempo markings and their translations:

- Adagio – slow

- Vivo – lively and brisk

- Lento – slow

- Molto – a lot

- Mosso – motion or movement

- Piu – more

- Allegro – fast

- (un) poco – a little

- Meno – less

Harmony

Harmony is the result of having more than one pitch being heard at the same time. When you hear two or more notes being played at one time, you are listening to harmony. Harmony provides support for the melody and gives it texture. Harmony is usually described as being diminished, augmented, major, and minor.

Melody

Melody can be described as the general tune that is created when you play a succession of notes. It is influenced by your rhythm and pitch. A musical piece can have just one melody running through it, or it may have several melodies stacked in a verse-chorus form.

Timbre

Timbre is the quality of a sound that differentiates one musical instrument or voice from another. It is also called *tone color*. Timbre has nothing to do with the volume, length, or pitch of a sound.

For example, if you play a specific note on a clarinet and then on an oboe for five seconds at a specific volume, a listener can easily know that the notes are different. This is because the timbre of a clarinet is different from that of an oboe.

Texture

This refers to the type and number of layers that are used in a musical composition. Texture can be a single melodic line (monophonic), several melodic lines (polyphonic), or the main melody together with chords (homophonic).

Dynamics

This is the intensity that a musical piece is performed. In written music, dynamics are represented by symbols or abbreviations that indicate the volume that a note should be sung or played. Just like tempo, dynamics are derived from Italian words. For example, *fortissimo* indicates an extremely loud passage while *pianissimo* indicates an extremely soft section of music.

Here are some typical dynamic markings:

- mf mezzo forte   = medium loud

- f   forte   = loud

- ff   fortissimo   = very loud

- fff fortississimo = very, very loud

- p   piano   = soft

- pp pianissimo   = very soft

- mp mezzo piano = medium soft

Exercise 3

1. Test yourself and see whether you can interpret what these Italian tempo markings mean:

   - Poco pin mosso

   - Piu vivo

   - Un poco allegro

   - Molto adagio

2. Write these dynamics in order from the quietest to the loudest: f, p, mf, ff, pp, and mp

Chapter Summary

Here are some of the key points you need to remember:

- Rhythm is the pattern of sounds repeated throughout the music.
- Rhythm depends on the tempo and beat of the music
- Tempo refers to the pace of the music and is usually indicated by Italian words.
- Harmony is created when more than one pitch is played at the same time.
- Melody is the general tune created when a succession of notes is played. A musical piece can have one or more melodies.
- Timbre is what tells us the difference between sounds made by different instruments.
- Texture is the number and type of layers in a musical composition. It can be monophonic, polyphonic, or homophonic.
- Dynamics is the intensity that music is played, and its markings are derived from Italian words.

In the next chapter, you will learn more about the different types of music scales. These are considered to be subsets of the notes you learned in Chapter 3.

Chapter Five: Forming Music Scales

In this chapter, you will learn how to create the different types of music scales. You will start with the simplest one, which is the major scale, and then proceed onto the more complex minor scale.

Music scales can be described as a set of notes arranged in sequential order, chosen to be used for a particular song. Why do we choose those notes? Simply because they sound great together! Though different cultures have adopted a variety of scales, the most common one is the major scale.

In order to create a scale, you need to go through the music alphabet (remember the seven letters from A to G?) and pick out notes that go well together. The notes chosen must achieve a particular sound. In most cases, you can do this by combining whole steps and half steps.

Tonal Centre

Every scale begins with the note that it is named after. That particular note is referred to as the ***tonal centre*** of that scale, and it is where the music in that scale feels "at rest."

For example, in most cases, music in the C major scale always ends on a C major chord. The music will begin on the C note, return to the C note repeatedly, and the melody will be based on the C note so much that listeners be able to identify where the tonal centre of that piece of music is.

Major Scales

If you have ever heard a song that sounds cheerful, uplifting, and fun, then it was probably written in a major key. Music that is written using a particular key only uses some of the many notes available. This sequence of notes then forms what we call a scale. Major keys are used to build major chords to then form a major scale.

It is important to know that different songs can use different scales, and different parts of a song can also make use of different scales. Scales are normally written in a sequential order from one note to the next note of the same letter. For example, we can have a scale that ranges from note C to the next note C, as shown below.

C D E F G A B C

As we already learned, each set of seven letters of the music alphabet forms an octave. Therefore, we can say that the above scale is a one-octave scale. To create a two-octave scale, you simply continue the same sequence until you land on the next note with the same letter name.

C D E F G A B C D E F G A B C

The range of notes from C to C is what forms the scale for C major. None of the notes in this particular scale has a sharp or a flat. On the other hand, the D major scale has two sharps. These are F sharp and C sharp.

D E F♯ G A B C♯ D

So, the question you are probably asking is: How are we supposed to know which notes should be sharpened and which ones should be flattened? The first method involves the use of a chart. However, this can be a cumbersome way since you have to keep referring all the time. You may even be forced to cram all that information into your head. The better alternative is to learn how to use whole and half steps.

Whole Steps and Half Steps

We talked about how the pitch of a sound represents how high or low the sound is. In music, we usually say that one note is either much higher or lower than another. This distance between two pitches is known as a half step. If you look at figure 5.1 below, you will be able to understand this better. This method of counting up whole and half steps can be used to form music scales from scratch.

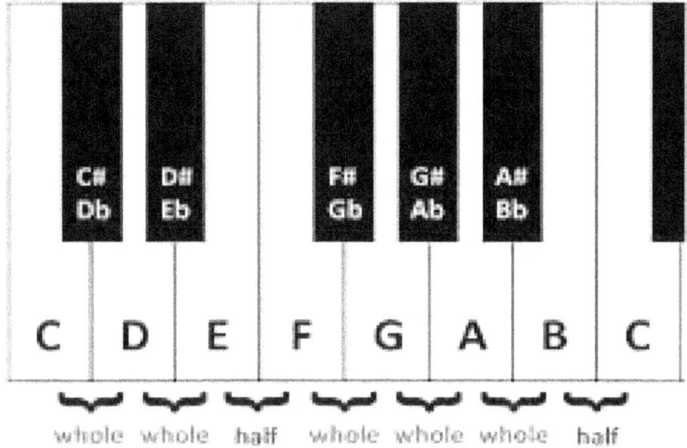

Figure 5.1

For example, we know that the distance from A to A♯ is a half step. The distance between B and B♭ is a half step. In other words, two consecutive half steps form a whole step. The format of any major scale usually follows this kind of sequence:

whole whole half whole whole whole half

This can also be written as:

w w h w w w h

This sequence means that there is a whole step between the first and second note, the second and third note, the fourth and fifth note, the fifth and sixth note, and the sixth and seventh note. There is a half step between the third and fourth note and the seventh and eighth note.

Please memorize this pattern because every major scale you encounter from here onwards will use this same sequence.

So, if we want to form the C major scale, we can write it as:

C w D w E h F w G w A w B h C

Figure 5.2

However, if we want to form the D major scale, we can write it as:

D w E w F♯ h G w A w B w C♯ h D

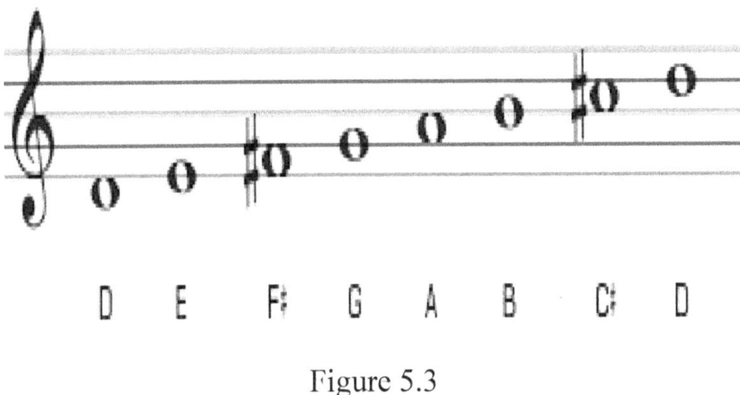

Figure 5.3

Minor Scales

Most people think of minor scales as confusing. This is because many music students usually start learning about the major scale first and end up focusing on it more than the minor scale. This situation isn't helped by the fact that there are a number of different types of minor scales that are often confused with one another. However, we will only focus on the most common minor scale in this book.

It is important to note that a piece of music in a particular major scale will sound the same as music in another major scale. For example, music that is in C major will sound somewhat similar to music in D major.

However, music in D major will sound very different from that in D minor because the notes in a minor scale are arranged in a very different pattern. Music written using a minor key has a sad, ominous, or mysterious sound than that written using a major key.

Natural Minor Scale

A natural minor scale is a scale where every note is played in a minor key signature. A natural minor scale is formed by starting at the tonal centre and moving upward using the following step pattern:

Whole half whole whole half whole whole

w h w w h w w

For example, music written in D minor scale will look like this:

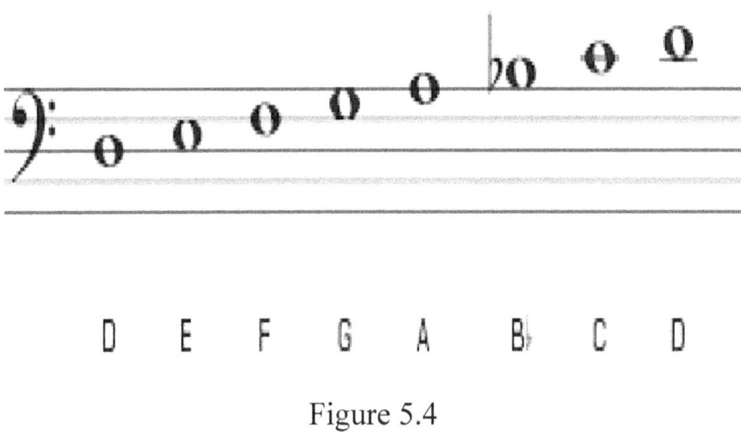

Figure 5.4

Exercise 4

1. Draw a staff with a treble clef. Write down the notes of the A major scale.

2. Draw a staff with a bass clef. Write down the notes of the G flat major scale.

3. Draw a staff with a treble clef. Write down the notes of the F minor scale.

4. Draw a staff with a treble clef. Write down the notes of the A flat minor scale.

Chapter Summary

Here are the key points to remember from this chapter:

- A music scale is a set of notes that sound good together, arranged in sequential order, within a particular piece of music.
- The tonal centre is the first note in a scale and is used to name that particular scale.
- To remember the sequence of notes in a major scale, follow the pattern *w w h w w w h.*
- A natural minor scale is written in a minor key and follows the pattern *w h w w h w w.*

In the next chapter, you will learn about the different types of intervals and how they are built.

Chapter Six: Building Intervals

In this chapter, you will learn about the different types of intervals and how to name them. Intervals are a very important concept in music. In fact, you cannot learn about scales or chords without making some reference to intervals. As a serious student of music theory, you must take the time to learn intervals and how to identify them.

Defining Intervals

An interval can be defined as the distance or space between two notes or pitches. Intervals are described using whole steps and half steps, which we have already covered in the previous chapters. The uncomplicated way to describe an interval would be to say, "E natural is one-half step below F natural," or "A flat is one step and a half away from F."

However, these are small distances. What about when we need to describe longer intervals in a major or minor scale?

How to Name Intervals

The primary factor you have to consider when naming an interval is the distance between the two notes. You need to look at how the notes are presented and then count the spaces and lines between the notes in the staff. Make sure that you include the spaces or lines that the notes are positioned on.

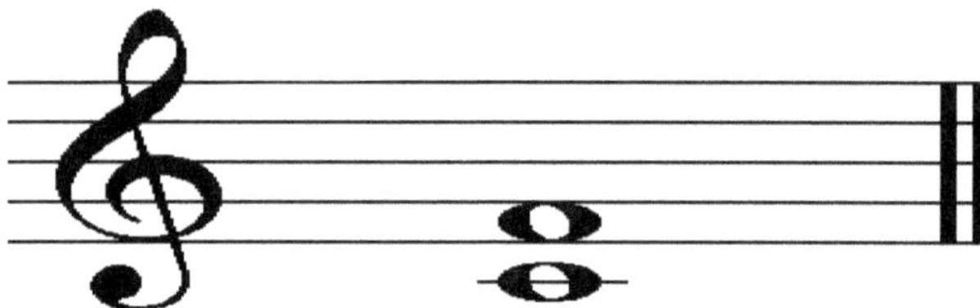

Figure 6.1

Figure 6.2

In figure 6.1 above, the interval between the C and F notes is four. We refer to this *a fourth*. In figure 6.2, the interval count between C and E is a third. At this point, the type of clef, key signature, and accidental (flats and sharps) don't matter.

If the interval between the notes is less or equal to one octave, it is referred to as a **simple interval** *(fig 6.3)*. If the interval is greater than one octave, it is called a **compound interval** *(fig 6.4)*.

Figure 6.3

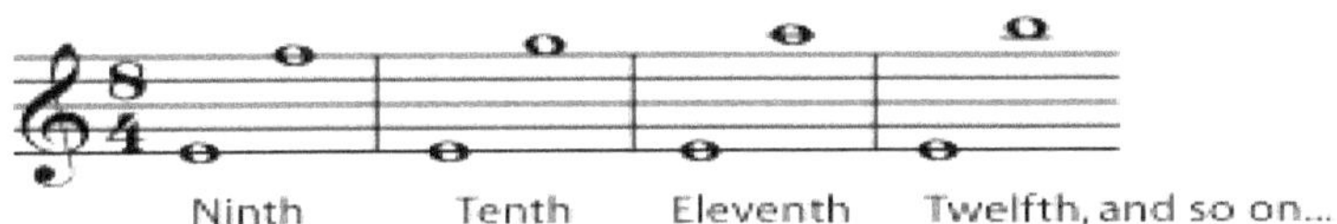

Figure 6.4

Now in the next phase of identifying an interval, we will consider the clef, key signature, and accidentals.

Perfect Intervals

Certain intervals are considered to be perfect intervals. They include primes, fourths, fifths, and octaves. They are called perfect because their sound waves are related very closely to one another. This makes these intervals sound good together.

Another name for a perfect prime is *unison,* which represents two notes that produce the same pitch. A perfect fourth has 5 half steps and a perfect fifth has 7 half steps. A perfect octave is where two notes are eight intervals apart, that is, 12 half steps apart. It is important that you understand how these steps are counted. You can go back and refresh your knowledge from the previous chapter on scales.

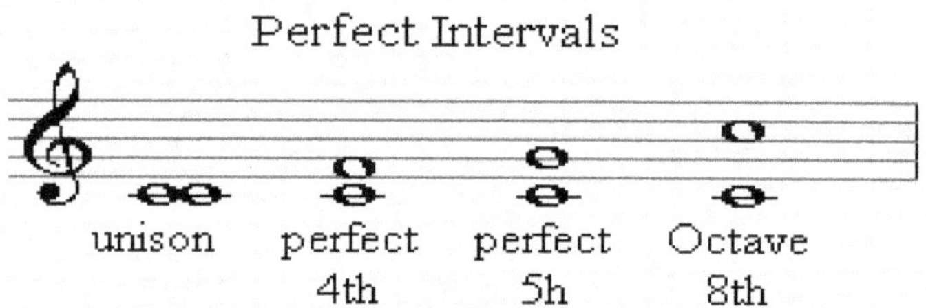

Figure 6.5

Major and Minor Intervals

The rest of the simple intervals form the major and minor intervals. These include seconds, thirds, sixths, and sevenths. A minor interval is one half-step smaller than a major one. They are described as follows:

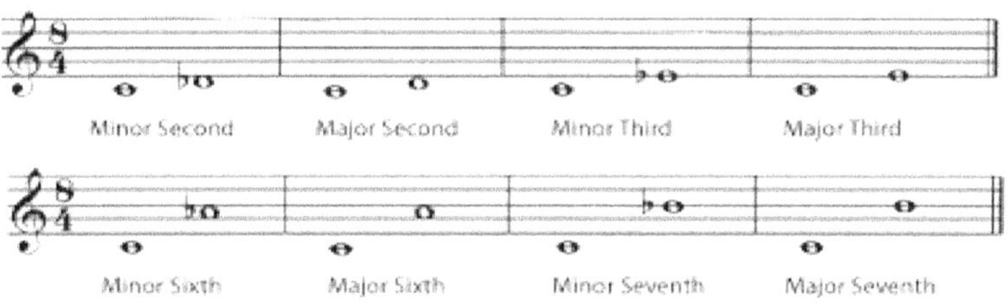

Figure 6.6

- Minor second – 1 half step

- Major second – 2 half steps

- Minor third – 3 half steps

- Major third – 4 half steps

- Minor sixth – 8 half steps

- Major sixth – 9 half steps

- Minor seventh – 10 half steps

- Major seventh – 11 half steps

57

Exercise 5

1. Give the complete name of the intervals.

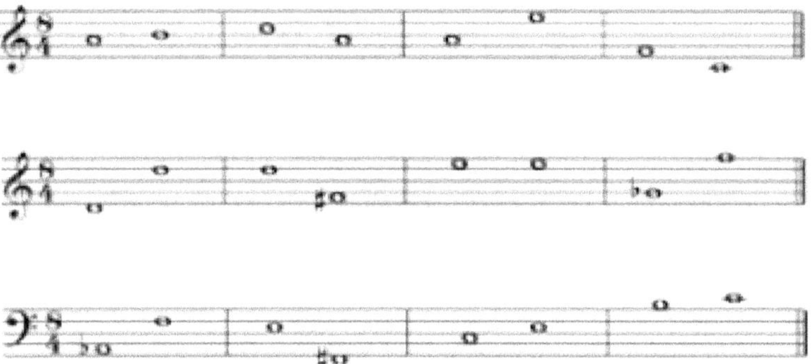

Chapter Summary

Here are the key points that you need to remember:

- Interval is the distance between two pitches.
- In order to name an interval, count the lines and spaces between the two notes. Don't forget to include the line or space the notes are standing on.
- The second phase of naming an interval must consider the half steps. The clef, key signature, and accidentals are important here.
- A simple interval is one octave or smaller, while a compound interval is greater than one octave.
- Intervals are considered perfect if their sound waves are closely related. Perfect intervals include primes, fourths, fifths, and octaves
- A perfect prime is also called unison.
- A minor interval is one half-step smaller than a major interval. These intervals include seconds, thirds, sixths, and sevenths.

In the next chapter, you will learn about key signatures and the circle of fifths.

Chapter Seven: Key Signatures

In this chapter, you will learn about how to use key signatures to make the performance of music much easier. You will also learn about the major and minor key signatures as well as how to read the circle of fifths.

Key signatures are a very important part of music. The key signature is what we use to know the pitches that a song will be performed. Every time that a piece of music is performed, it is played in a particular key or tonality. For example, if a song is to be played using the D key, then the entire song must be based around a D chord or a D note. Even the notes used will be from a D scale. The key signature represents all this information.

So how do we know the key that is being used?

If you look at the beginning of every line of written music, you will notice that there are sharps or flats (also known as accidentals) right after the clef symbol. These accidentals tell us the key to use. It is important to note that a key can either be a sharp or a flat, but it can never be both.

So, what is the significance of using keys? When you are writing a long piece of music in a single key, you will soon find it very tedious to keep repeating the accidentals all over the staff. Look at the image below to see what a simple melody in D major looks like if you don't use a key signature.

Figure 7.1

Now, this is just a short section of a piece of music. If you were writing a full song, the staff would get quite messy, not to mention the fact that you would get tired of writing all those sharps. So, to avoid this, music composers use key signatures only at the beginning of the staff to show the performers which pitches must have accidentals.

Below is the same simple melody in D major. But this time it has a key signature that indicates that the notes C and F should be sharpened.

Figure 7.2

The Circle of Fifths

This is a graphical way of arranging keys to show how closely related they are to each other. The circle of fifths has been part of music theory for centuries, and it provides a great method for summarizing the key signatures to be used for any key that has a maximum of seven sharps or flats.

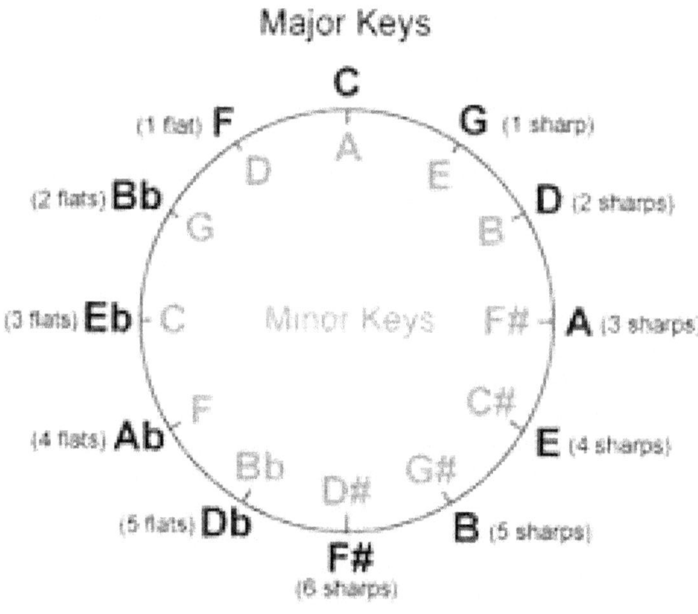

Figure 7.3

So how will you know which notes in the key are supposed to be sharpened or flattened? In order to use the circle of fifths to identify your key signature, you must use a mnemonic device to help you memorize the order of sharps and flats.

The first thing to do is memorize the order of notes on the following circle:

F C G D A E B

Most people use the mnemonic *Father Charles Goes Down And Ends Battle*

If you want to determine the sharp keys, you move clockwise around the circle of fifths. Then you read the mnemonic forward. For example, according to the circle of fifths, there are three sharps in the key A major. But which notes exactly are supposed to be sharp?

Moving clockwise along the circle and following the order of notes, you will identify the notes to be sharpened as F, C, and G.

If you want to determine the flat keys, you must move anticlockwise along the circle, and then read the mnemonic backward. For example, according to the circle of fifths, there are four flats in the key for A-flat major. But which notes should be flattened?

Moving anticlockwise along the circle and backward along the order of notes, you will see that B, E, A, and D are the notes that will have flats.

The reason why we call it a circle of fifths is because as you move from one section (or key) to the next, you are moving down or up by an interval of a perfect fifth. If you move clockwise by a perfect fifth, you will land on a key with one sharp more or one flat less than where you started. If you move anticlockwise a perfect fifth, you land on a key that has one flat more or one sharp less than where you started.

Minor Key Signatures

So far, we have been focusing more on the major keys. However, minor keys also have signatures. Every major key you see on the circle of fifths has a corresponding minor key with the exact same signature. Minor and major keys that have corresponding key signatures are referred to as ***relative keys***. For example, both F major and D minor have one flat. F major is regarded as the relative major of D minor while D minor is regarded as the relative minor of F major.

In other words, just because keys are next to each other on a keyboard (the chromatic scale) does not mean that they are closely related. The main factor that determines the relationship is having similar key signatures. The closer the keys are in the circle of fifths, the closer their relationship in terms of key signature.

This means that the next most closely related keys to F major and D minor are C major (or A minor), and B major (or G minor). Those keys that don't correspond at all with the key signature of F major are on the opposite side of the circle.

Exercise 6

1. Which keys in the circle of fifths are closely related to F sharp major and B flat major?

2. Name the major and minor keys for each key signature.

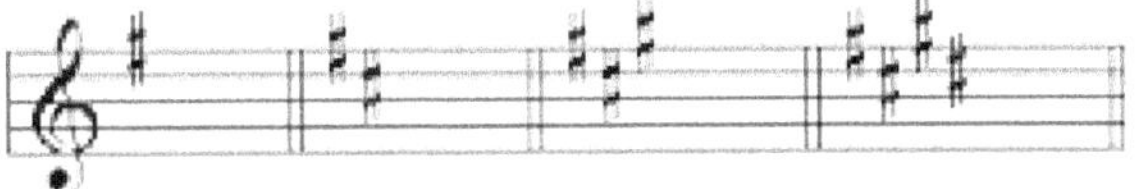

Chapter Summary

Here are the key points to remember:

- Key signatures tell us the pitches that a song will be performed in.
- To make writing music much easier, the key signature is placed at the beginning of the staff instead of between the notes in the staff.
- The accidentals indicate the key to be used in a piece of music.
- The circle of fifths is a graphical illustration of keys and indicates how closely related they are to each other.
- To determine the key being used, look at the number of sharps or flats in the key signature.
- To identify key signatures, use the mnemonic Father Charles Goes Down And Ends Battle (FCGDAEB).
- To identify the sharp keys, move clockwise around the circle and read the mnemonic forwards.
- To identify the flat keys, move anticlockwise and read the mnemonic backward.
- Major and minor keys that have corresponding key signatures are known as relative keys.

In the next chapter, you will learn about triads, chords, and chord progressions.

Chapter Eight: Building Chords

In this chapter, you will learn chords, which are the building blocks of the tone of a piece of music. Learning how to build chords can be a bit challenging for beginners, but the trick lies in taking it one step at a time. For that reason, we are going to focus on building triads, major chords, and minor chords.

Chords

A chord is simply a group of notes that are played together. Most of the sad songs you hear use what are known as minor chords. The upbeat songs tend to use suspended second chords or major seventh chords. Chords can either be used to make melodies or they can be arranged in specific sequences known as progressions to create a sense of direction and movement in music.

Triads

Chords are a set of three or more pitches that are played together. A chord that is made up of three notes that can be arranged as thirds is known as a *triad*. The fastest way to know if a chord of three notes is a triad is to arrange the notes in a circle of thirds. If the pitch classes of the three notes sit next to each other, then they form a triad.

There are two ways of identifying a triad, i.e., according to its root and its quality. The *root of chord,* which is the note that gives the chord its name, is the lowest note. The second note in the triad is known as the *third of chord*, while the last note in the triad is called the *fifth of chord*. After you position the root of chord, you then place the third of chord a third higher than the root. The fifth of chord is then placed a fifth higher than the root, which coincides with a third higher than the third of chord. If you find this confusing, you may need to go to Chapter 6 (figure 6.3) where we learned about intervals.

In the figure below, the chord is written in the root position as a stack of third, which is the easiest way to write down a triad. Don't forget that in most cases, the root is the bottom note, unless you are dealing with an inversion.

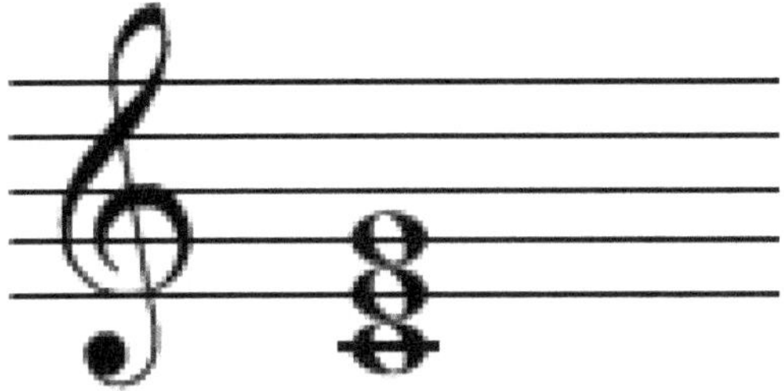

Figure 8.1

First and Second Inversions

First inversion occurs when the third of chord becomes the lowest note. In case the fifth of chord is placed at the bottom, then the chord is said to be in *second inversion*. The second inversion is also known as a *six-four chord* because the intervals are a sixth and a fourth.

The most important factor in a chord is not the distance between the top two notes from the lowest note. The number of notes also isn't an issue. The thing that matters the most is which note is at the bottom.

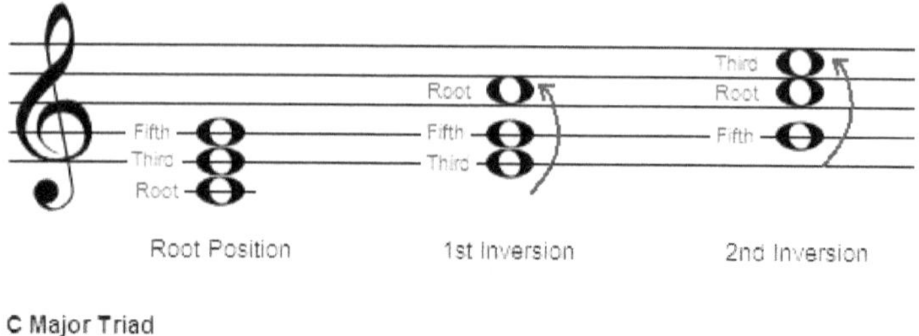

Figure 8.2

Triad Qualities

The first step in determining the quality of a triad is to identify the interval between the root and the other notes in the chord. The four qualities of triads that can be found in major and minor scales include:

- Major triad – M3 and P5 above root

- Minor triad – m3 and p5 above root

- Diminished triad – m3 and d5 above root

- Augmented triad – M3 and A5 above root

The two most common triads are the major and minor chords. In these two types of chords, the root of the chord and fifth of chord are at an interval of a perfect fifth, which are 7 half steps. This interval can be split into a major third, which is 4 half-steps, and a minor third, which forms 3 half-steps.

A ***major chord*** is formed when the major third falls between the root and the third of chord. A ***minor chord*** is formed when the minor third falls between the root and the third of chord.

On the other hand, diminished and augmented chords do not have a perfect fifth, which explains why they produce an anxious feeling in listeners. **Augmented chords** are formed when two major thirds are combined, thus creating an augmented fifth. **D*iminished chords*** are formed when two minor thirds are combined, thus creating a diminished fifth.

Figure 8.3

Seventh Chords

This is a chord that is formed when you take a triad and combine it with a note that is a seventh above the root. There are many different varieties of seventh chords, and we distinguish them according to the type of seventh and type of triad used. Here are some of the most common types of seventh chords:

- Dominant seventh chord – This is a combination of a major triad and a minor seventh

- Minor seventh chord – This is a combination of a minor triad and a minor seventh

- Major seventh chord – This is a combination of a major triad and a major seventh

- Diminished seventh chord – This is a combination of a diminished triad and a diminished seventh

- Half-diminished seventh chord – This is a combination of a diminished triad and a minor seventh

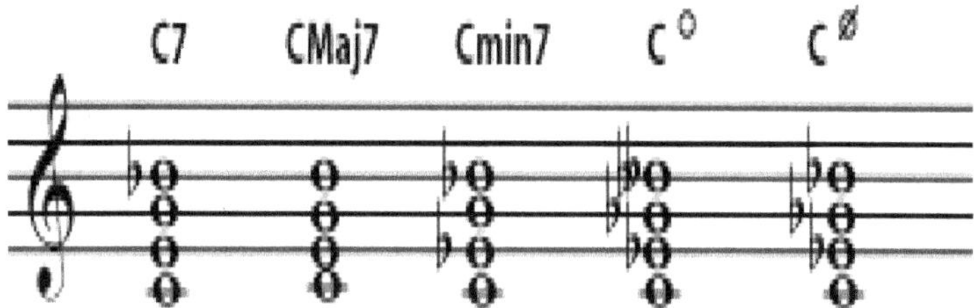

Figure 8.4

Exercise 7

1. Write these seventh chords – G minor seventh; B flat major seventh; F sharp minor seventh; and D diminished seventh.

Chapter Summary

Here are some of the key points that you need to remember:

- A chord is a group of notes that are played together.
- A chord that comprises three notes arranged as thirds is known as a triad.
- Its root and quality can identify a triad.
- In a triad, the lowest note is the root of chord; the second note is the third of chord, and the last note is the fifth of chord.
- First inversion occurs when the third of chord becomes the lowest note.
- Second inversion occurs when the fifth of chord becomes the lowest note.
- When the interval between the root and third of chord is the major third, a major chord is formed.
- When the interval between the root and third of chord is the minor third, a major chord is formed.
- When two major thirds are combined, an augmented chord is formed.

- When two minor thirds are combined, a diminished chord is formed.
- A seventh chord is formed when you add a triad and a note that is a seventh above the root.

Final Words

You have come to the end of the book. Though it was a long journey, I'm sure you now have a much better understanding of music theory than before. If you had never studied the subject previously, you should be ready to move on to the more complex theories of music. If you already had a background in music, then your knowledge of music theory will help you become an even better musician. For those who were seeking a refresher course in some of the elements you had forgotten, consider your mind refreshed.

Music theory is not really as hard as it looks or sounds. The bottom line is that you have to have a solid foundation that will always be there to guide you. The seven elements of music we have covered in this book are the keys to unlocking any musical composition. On top of that, there are seven good exercises in this book that will help you crystallize the knowledge you have gained in each chapter.

The questions provided in every exercise have covered the fundamentals that every music student and musician must know like the back of their hand. If you were keen when reading the book, I'm sure you had an easy time answering them. If you felt like you were struggling a little bit, then don't worry about it. Just go back to the chapter where you feel uncertain and reread it. Some of the concepts usually take time to sink in. Don't forget that the answers to every question are on the last page of the book.

Being able to read and write music is a very rewarding experience, and now you are ready to move onto the next phase of your musical journey. Yes, that was the easy part. Anybody can buy a book, read it, and toss it aside. All it will cost you is some time and money. However, you must now do the hard work necessary to integrate and incorporate this new knowledge into your music. This book has provided you with an opportunity to learn something that can help you going forward. Don't stop here. What is important is that you continue to practice and challenge yourself. Never stop learning and always make an effort to put into practice everything that you have learned in this book.

I am honoured that you took the time to read this book. It was a pleasure for me to walk with you through your musical journey. I hope you enjoyed reading and learning from this beginner's guide to music theory.

Thank you and good luck!

Solutions to Exercise Questions

Solutions to Exercise 1

1. Draw the staff on a piece of paper and practice writing the two clef symbols on the staff. Draw as many as you can until you learn it perfectly.

2. Draw the staff with a treble clef and name all the spaces on the staff.

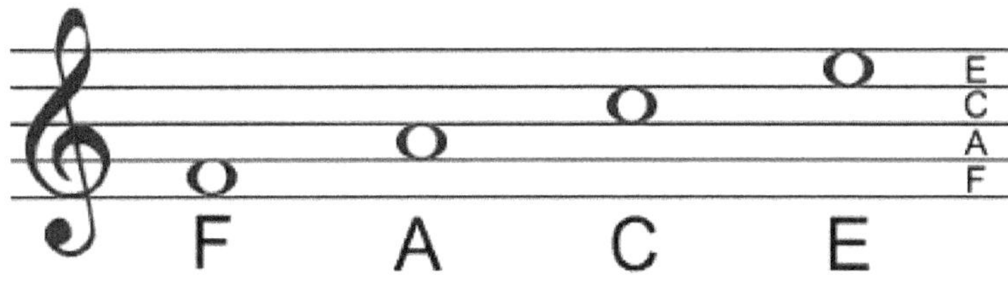

3. Draw the staff with a bass clef and name all the lines on it.

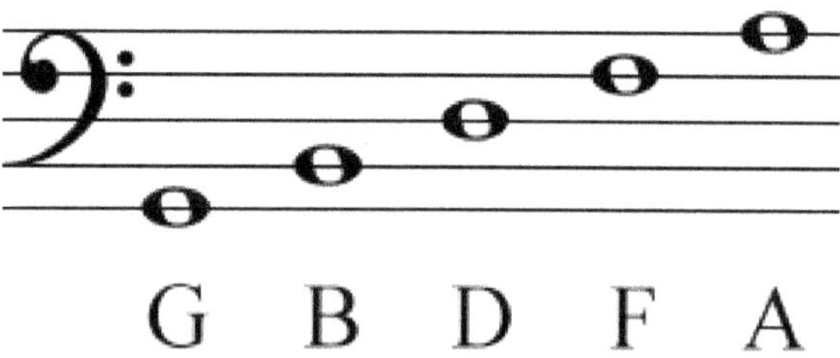

4. On a staff with a treble clef, name the ledger lines and spaces above the staff.

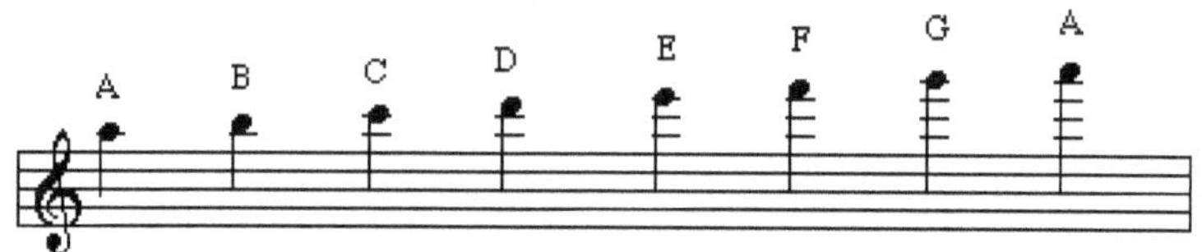

5. On a staff with a bass clef, name the ledger lines and spaces below the staff.

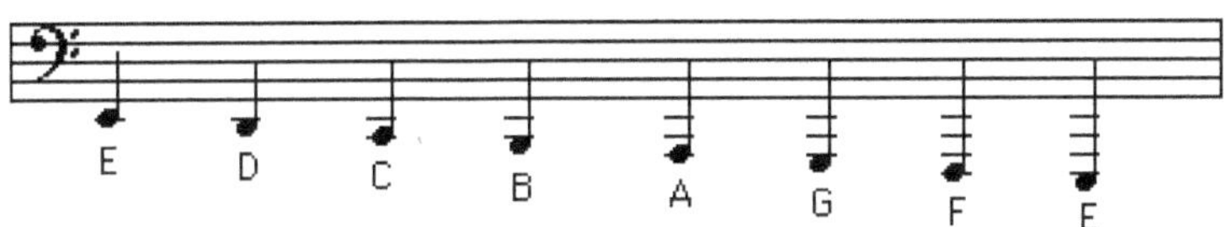

E
D
C
B
A
G
F
E

Solutions to Exercise 2

1. Complete the following series of natural notes: A B C D
    E F G A

2. Provide an alternative name for the following:

A♯ - B ♭

D♭ - C♯

G♭ - F♯

E♭ - D♯

3. 1 semibreve = 8 quavers

4. 1 minim = 4 quarters

5. 1 minim = 1 quarter + 2 eighths

6. Three staves with a treble clef symbol and time
    signatures showing *two four time, three eight time,* and
    six four time. Fill in each measure with a different
    combination of note lengths. Use at least one dotted note
    per staff.

Solutions to Exercise 3

1. Italian tempo markings:

   - Poco piu mosso – a little more movement/motion

   - Piu vivo – more lively

   - Un poco allegro – a little fast

   - Molto adagio – very slow

2. In order from quietest to loudest: pp, mp, p, f, mf, ff

Solutions to Exercise 4

1. The staff with a treble clef and notes of the A major scale.

2. The staff with a bass clef and notes of the G flat major scale.

G-flat major scale

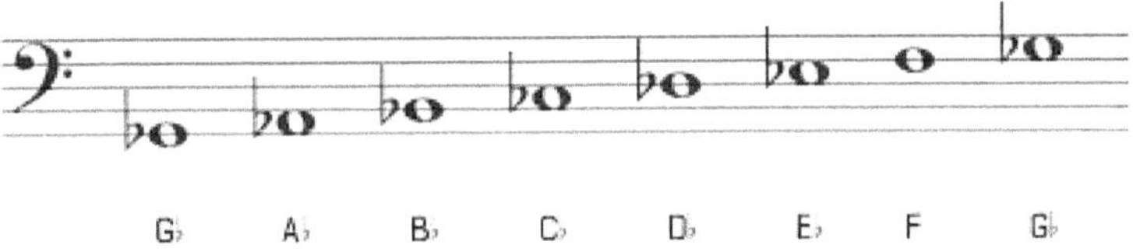

3. The staff with a treble clef and notes of the F minor scale.

F minor scale

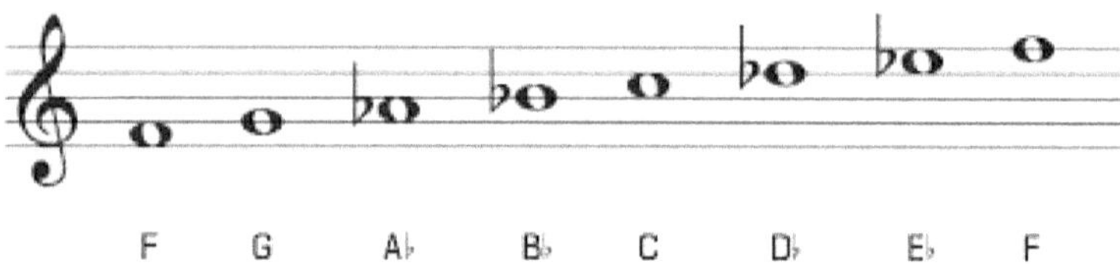

4. The staff with a treble clef and notes of the A flat minor scale.

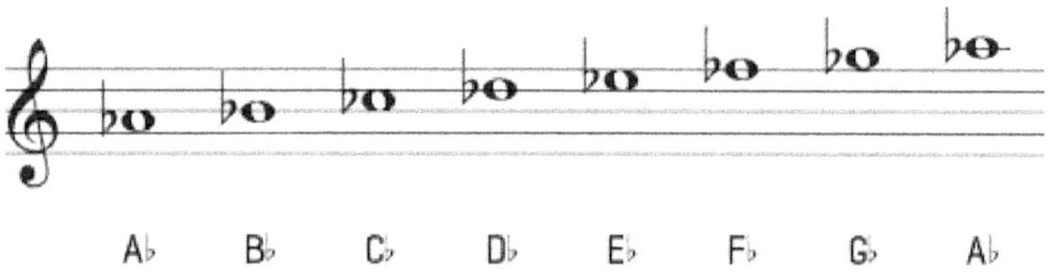

Solutions to Exercise 5

Names of intervals:

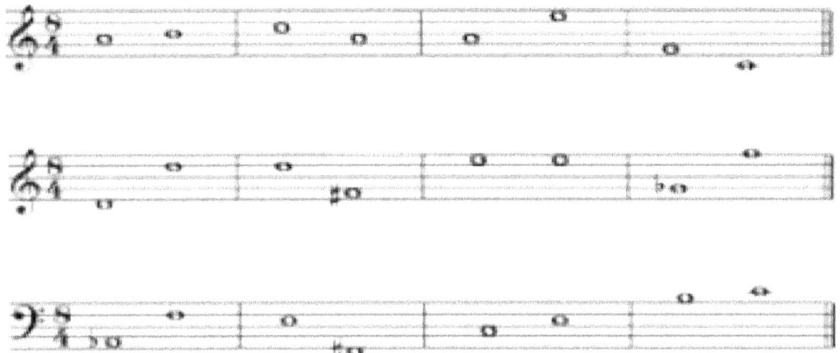

Top Staff:

Major Second - Minor Third - Perfect Fifth - Perfect Fourth

Centre Staff:

Perfect Octave – Minor Sixth – Perfect Prime (Unison) –
Major Seventh

Bottom Staff:

Major Sixth – Minor Seventh – Major Third – Minor Second

Solution to Exercise 6

1. Relative keys to:

F sharp major – D sharp minor

B flat major – G minor

2. Major and minor keys for each key signature:

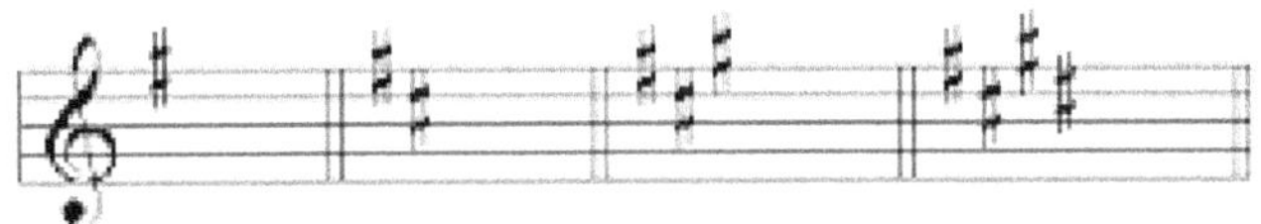

G Major – D Major – A Major – E Major

Solutions to Exercise 7

G minor 7th chord

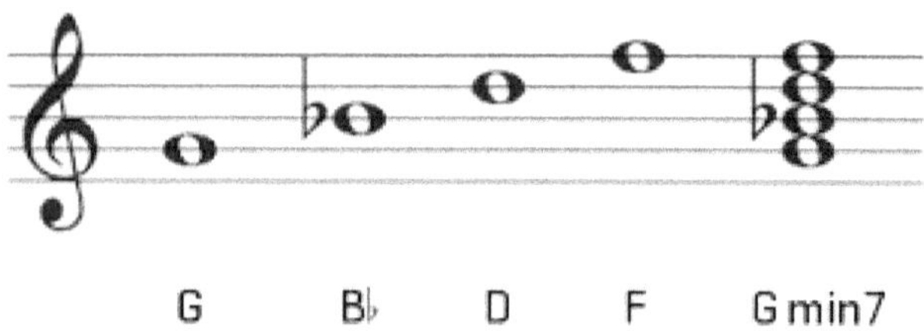

B-flat major 7th chord

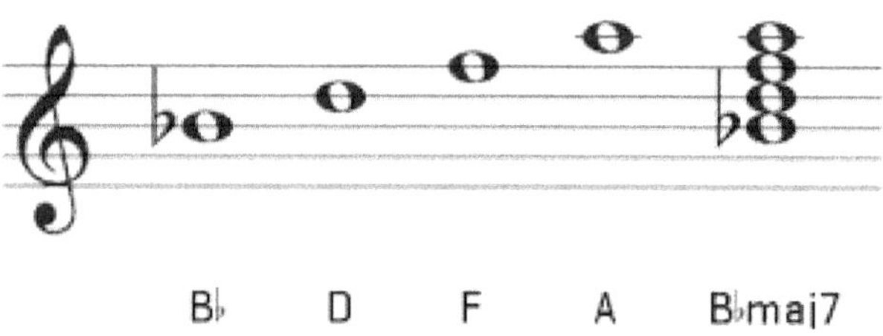

F-sharp minor 7th chord

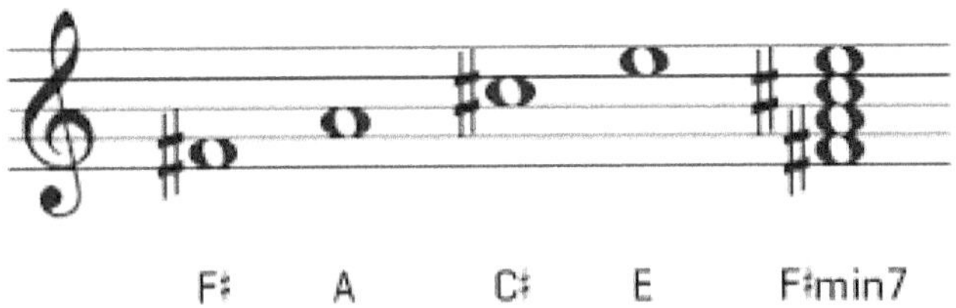

D diminished 7th chord

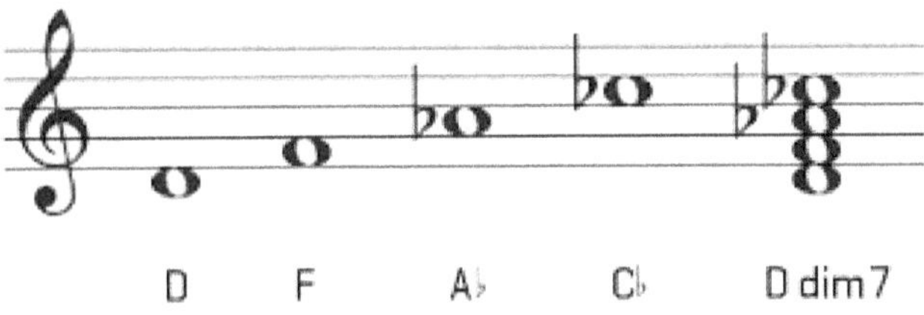

HOW TO PLAY
GUITAR
IN 1 DAY
The Only 7 Exercises You Need to
Learn Guitar Chords, Guitar Scales
and Guitar Tabs Today
PRESTON HOFFMAN

BOOK 2

HOW TO PLAY GUITAR: IN 1 DAY

The Only 7 Exercises You Need to Learn Guitar Chords, Guitar Scales and Guitar Tabs Today

Preston Hoffman

Table of Contents

Introduction

Thank you for purchasing this book. You are now already on your way to becoming a guitarist.

The guitar is one of the most versatile instruments that there is and one of the most straightforward to play. Becoming a player opens you to a world of fun, relaxation and satisfaction.

For some, it might lead to a bit of extra income, if you join a band. Making music is a wonderful thing; making it in the company of others is even better.

By buying this book, you have made the first move to acquiring lifelong skills, which will provide much laughter, much joy and immense satisfaction.

We suggest that you work through this book a chapter at a time, spending long enough in each lesson to have secured the skills before moving on to the next chapter. It may seem hard at the outset, but it will quickly become easier.

This is a very practical book. You will be playing straight away. There are two useful chapters at the end, which offer more detail on questions that might arise, and a glossary of terms. There are also some songs to get you playing.

Mostly, this book will introduce you to playing the guitar. Give yourself a day, and you will be well on your way.

Chapter One: Getting Started – Lesson One - The Parts of the Guitar, and How to Hold It

The saying goes that there is no time like the present, so if your aim is to learn to play the guitar quickly, let us get straight into it.

Essential Information

A few notes, though, before we start. There is a glossary at the back of this book. Any term followed by an asterisk (*) will be defined in the alphabetical glossary at the end.

Secondly, a very useful tip is to get your head around each chapter before moving on to the next. The better understanding you have of each section, the more rapid your progress will be.

In addition, the learning will stick, and you will not have to constantly look back to re-learn the skills that this book will help you to acquire.

Next, don't worry if you get sore fingers on your left (fret*) hand, especially if you are playing a steel string guitar. The skin on the end of your fingers will quickly harden and the soreness will disappear.

OK, let's get on with it. For the purposes of the rest of the chapter, the assumption is made that you already have your guitar, and that it is stringed and tuned*. If not, there are sections on choosing your guitar, stringing it and tuning the instrument later in the book.

The Parts of the Guitar

The guitar is formed from a few basic parts, each of which has their individual role. It doesn't really matter which kind of guitar you own, because the make-up is the same. If you have an electric guitar, there will be extra knobs and levers, but we will look at these later.

Guitar Head and Tuning Pegs

The head has two primary purposes. It is there to help sustain, or lengthen, the sound of the strings.

If you put your hand on the head, and play the open* strings with the other hand, you will sense the vibrations of the notes continuing to make a sound.

The second role of the head is hold the tuning pegs. These are the pegs connected to the rollers around which the strings are held tight. Turning these pegs changes the note. See the section on 'tuning' for more details.

Heads look different on the various types of guitar; do not worry about this, as they all perform the same task.

Guitar Neck and Nut

The picture above shows the nut. This is the part of the that holds the strings in place.

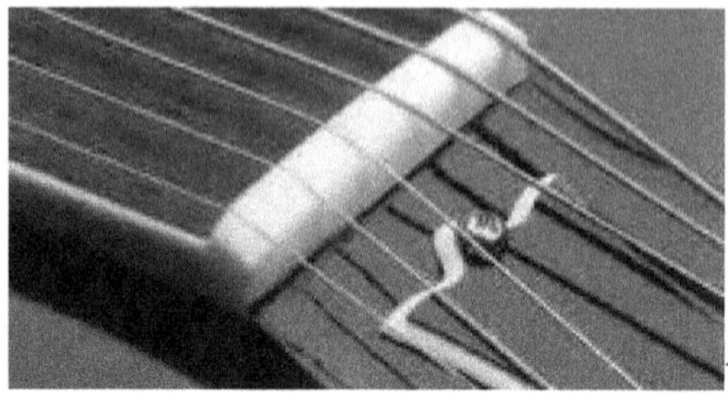

The nut has six little slots into each of which a string fits. It ensures that a full sound is heard by keeping the string away from the neck and frets.

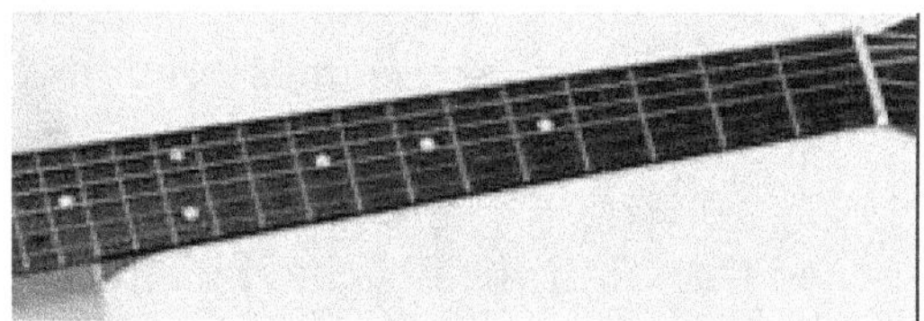

The picture above shows the neck of a guitar. This is the long section on which the frets are located. The example above has fret markers – the little dots that help the player to locate the appropriate fret when playing down the neck, which is more difficult than playing up at the head end. Not all guitars have these markers.

Here we can see the body of the guitar. The hole in the middle is called the sound hole, which is there to amplify the sound of the guitar. Electric guitars do not have these, as they have pick-ups (raised metal bars) to send the vibrations electronically to the amplifier.

Note that the body shape of a guitar can take many forms, especially with electric guitars. The final part of the guitar to identify is the bridge, into which the ends of the strings are fitted.

Holding the Guitar

As a beginner, it is best to start with a sitting position. As players become more experienced, then it is possible to play standing up, but the extra support offered when sitting helps the new player.

The position above is the classical stance when playing the Spanish* guitar. Note that the left foot is raised. A footrest can be purchased to facilitate this, but a pile of books or a block of wood works just as well. The guitar sits on the left leg, with the right just offering support. Both hands then fit into the natural position.

For larger guitars, such as acoustics*, then the picture below offers a more usual position. Here, the guitar is on the right leg, with the two legs close together. Of the two, the better one for the beginner is the Spanish guitar position. However, comfort is the most important thing of all.

Chapter Summary

So now we have the basics.

- You know the names of the parts of the guitar
- You know how to hold the instrument

In the next chapter you will begin to learn how to play.

Chapter Two: Lesson Two - Chords

In this chapter we will learn about the basic chords* which will allow you to begin to play songs almost immediately.

For a right-handed person, or somebody who plays right handed (most people do…) chords are formed with the left hand. Many songs can be played with just a collection of three or four chords, and in this chapter, we will look at the main ones.

There are seven notes in music, and chords are named after these. Chords are MAJOR* chords unless otherwise stated. Major chords make a kind of complete sound, whereas the other main form, MINOR* chords, make a sort of questioning, unfinished sound. Once you play one of each, the difference will be clear.

There are numerous varieties after that, but for this book, as it is for beginners, we will stick to just one alternative, a 7th chord*. This is a chord with an extra note (a seventh above the base note, for those interested).

The chords below are the ones that appear most commonly. Some, such as for example, the B Major chord (B) will appear in later chapters because they require a barre to play.

A Chords

Here, the lowest E string is not strummed*, the other five strings are. Use your first finger to cover the four strings on the second fret, then press the bottom string with your little finger

A

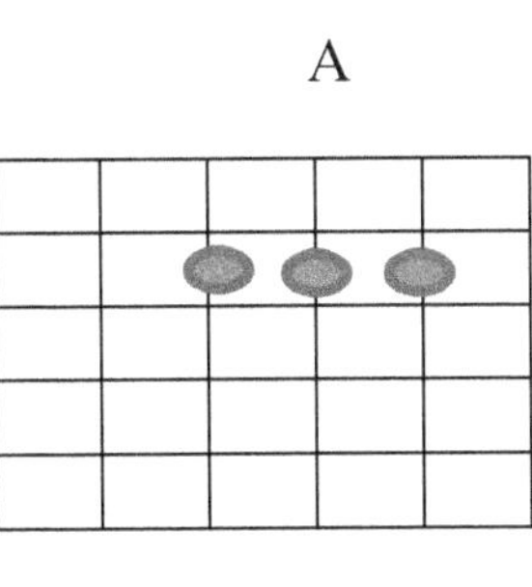

Am (A minor)

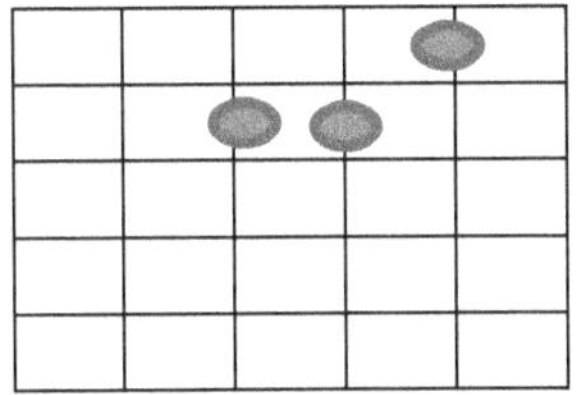

A7

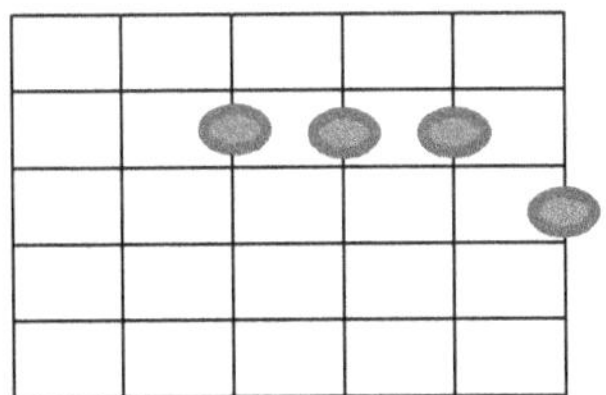

Use your first finger to cover the four strings on the second fret, then press the bottom string with your little finger

Am7

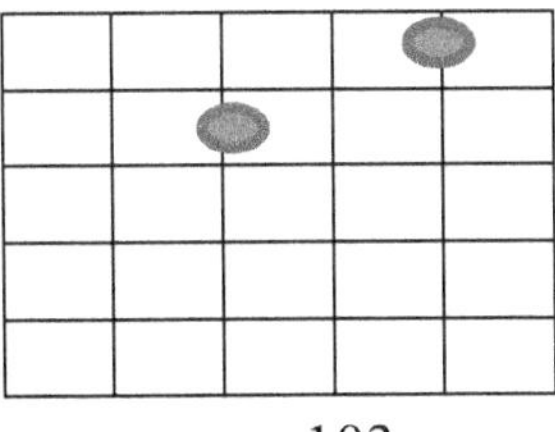

C Chords

As with A chords, the lowest E string is not strummed.

C

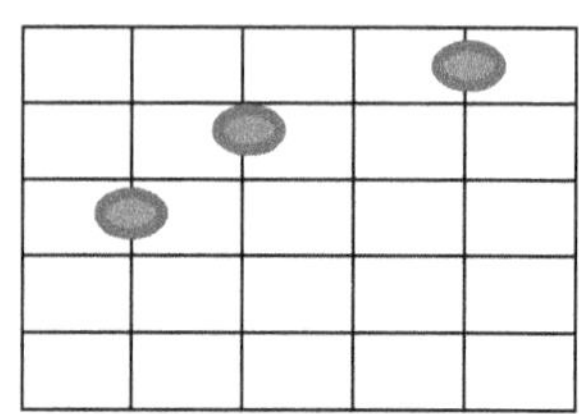

C7

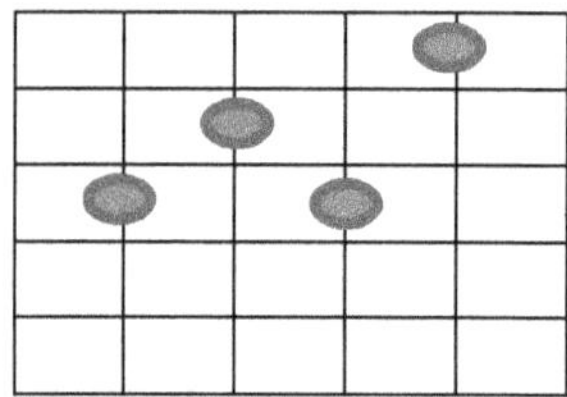

D Chords

Here, the lowest two strings, E and A, are not strummed.

D

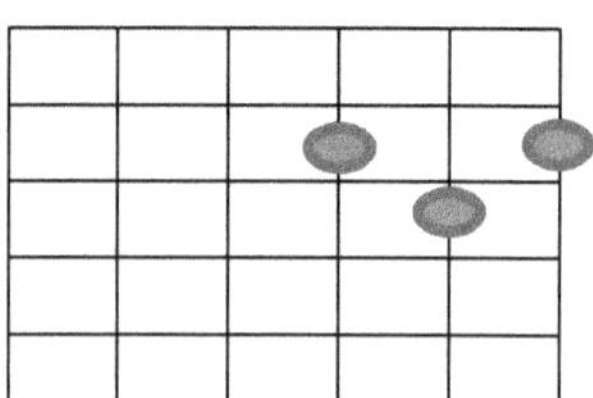

Dm

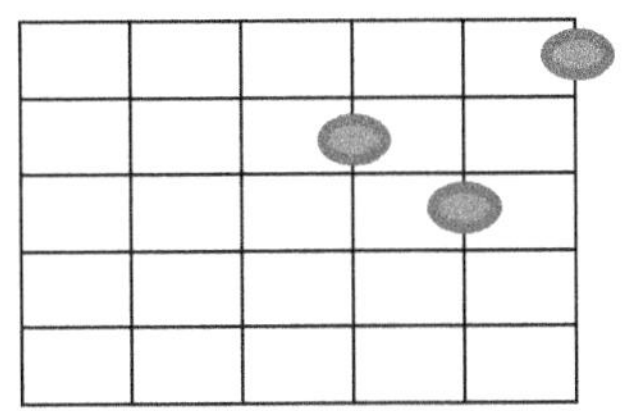

D7

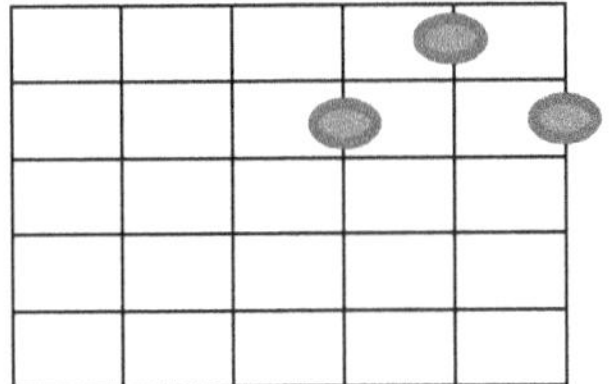

Dm7

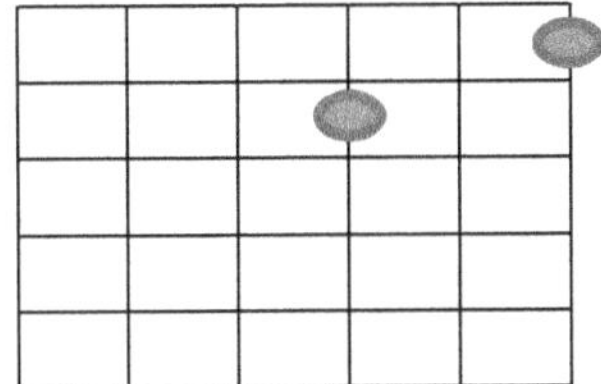

E Chords

Here, all strings are strummed.

E

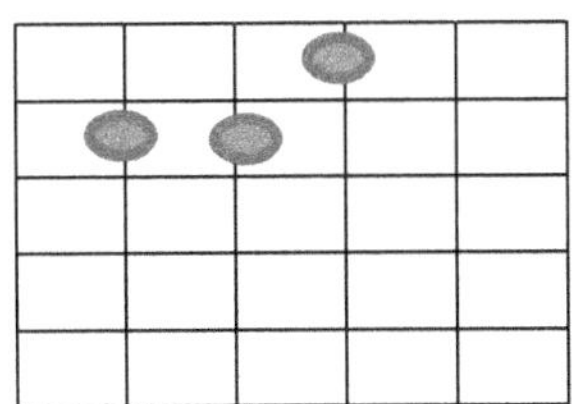

$$Em$$

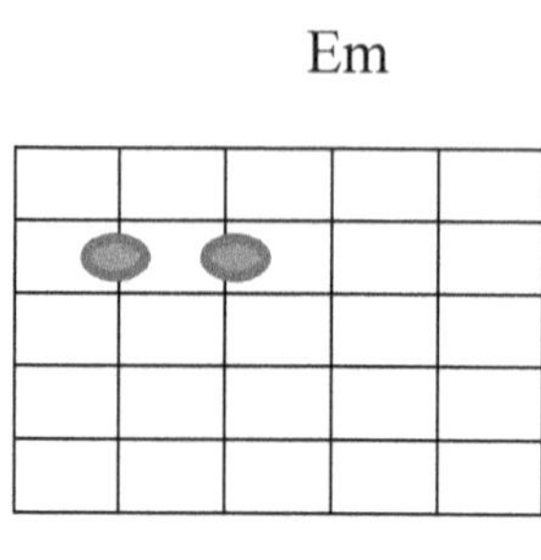

$$E7$$

Use your first finger to cover the four strings on the second fret, then press the bottom string with your little finger

$$Em7$$

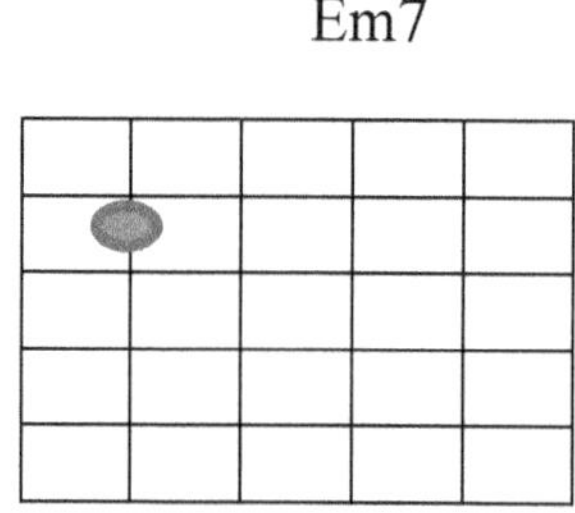

F Chords

If a barre is used, all strings are strummed, if not then the E and A strings are not strummed.

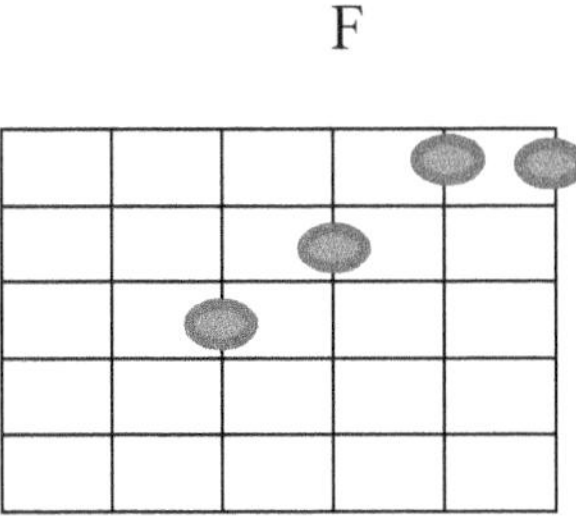

F

Use your first finger to hold down the first two strings. If you can, the first finger can create a bar by stretching over all six strings. It takes a bit of strength, but that soon develops.

G Chords

All strings are strummed.

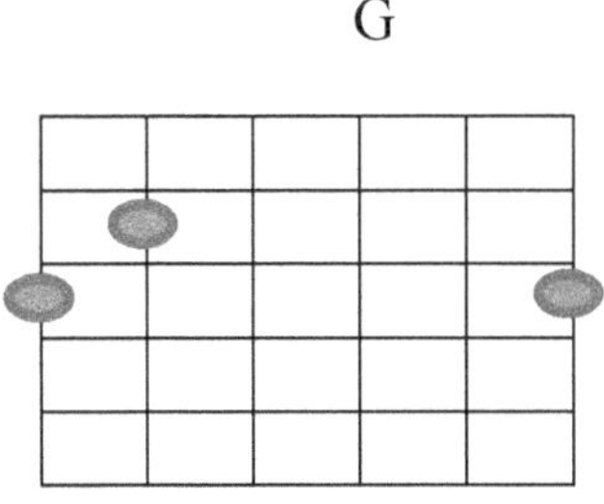

G

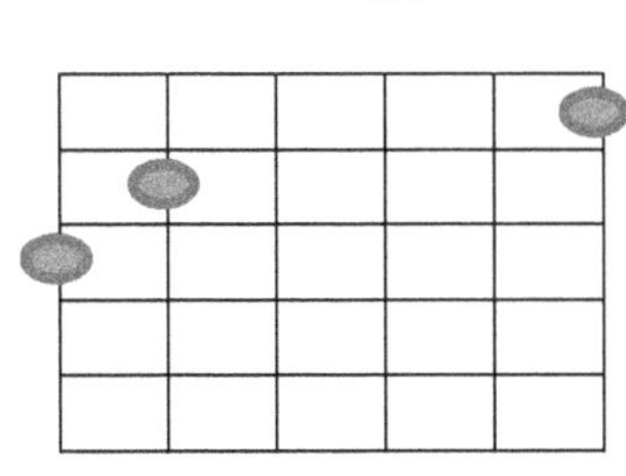

G7

The key with these chords is to practice them. Get them so that you can form each chord and play them so that there is no buzzing of the strings, or 'flat' sounds of a string not being pushed down firmly enough.

Progressions

Songs are often built around chord progressions. These are chords that simply go together well. Practice these and you will be able to use them in a wide range of songs.

The Most Common Progression

This works in any key, but for our purposes we will practice C, F and G

C C C C F F F F G G G G C C C C

Songs such as John Lennon's Imagine follow this progression.

Pop Progressions

These chord combinations work in popular songs such as Someone Like You by Adele. The chords are C, G, Am and F.

C C C C G G G G Am Am Am Am F F F F C C C C etc

Jazz Progressions

Everything from Boyfriend, the Justin Bieber, ummm, song and some of Queen's Bohemian Rhapsody follow this progression, which features the chords Dm, G and C.

Dm Dm Dm Dm G G G G C C C C Dm Dm Dm Dm etc

The Progression from the Fifties

Common in fact from the 1940s to the 1960s for both ballads and more upbeat songs, there are two progressions here. Firstly, is C Am Dm and G and songs such as the Beatles' The Fool on the Hill used this.

C C C C Am Am Am Am Dm Dm Dm Dm G G G G C C C C

Similar to this is the second progression which was used by the late great Leonard Cohen in the much-recorded Hallelujah. Here, the chords of C Am F and G are used.

C C C C Am Am Am Am F F F F G G G G

Chapter Summary

In this Chapter, we have presented all the most common chords that do not require a barre.

- These chords come in the major form, which is usually known just by its letter, that is, C is the same as C major
- They come in a seventh form
- The can also come in a minor form as well as a minor seventh version

- Chords are often put together in what are called progressions, and which form the basis of many songs.

In the next chapter you will learn a little bit about strumming.

Chapter Three: Lesson Three - Strumming

Before reading any further, give yourself a bit of a treat. Put your favourite CD, record, iPod song or whatever on to play. Listen carefully to the rhythm and count the beats of the drum. Sometimes, you can hear this on the guitars as well, but the drum is usually clearest.

What you are listening to is the beat of the song, sometimes called the time signature. In other words, the number of beats in a bar of music. If you learn to read music, this will be very important to help you play, but for the moment, just understanding about different rhythms in the simplest form is all that is needed.

Tap along to the beat, get that rhythm in your bones. What you will notice is that most, but not all, songs are written in 4/4 timing, that means that there are four beats in the bar. They might be played as eight quick beats, or two heavy and two light ones, or just 1,2,3,4; by counting or tapping your foot along you will see that the song is divided into blocks of four.

There are other rhythms, 3/4 is the beat of the waltz – **dum**, dee, dee, **dum**, dee, dee, **dum**, dee, dee, **dum**, dee, dee, etc. But we will start with four beats to the bar.

One tool here that can be very useful is a metronome, which is a device which ticks a steady rhythm out. You can buy a modern digital one from about $16, or a traditional one with a lever for about $100, which also makes a great ornament.

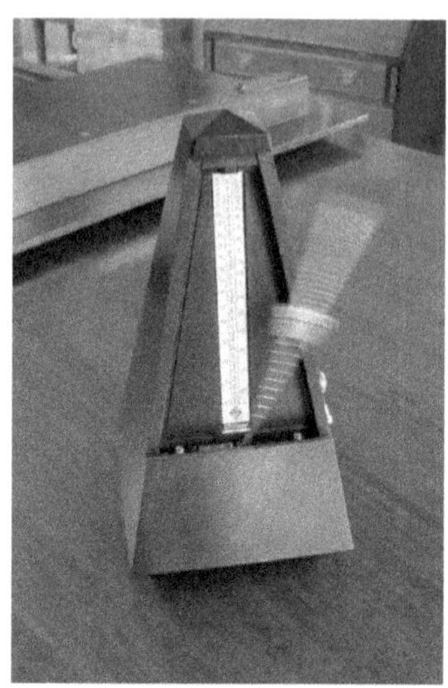

Or, there are apps available for your phone and free online versions. What the metronome will do, as it clicks away at the speed you set, is to help you keep a constant beat. This is really important as the guitar frequently supplies the rhythm for a song.

Basic Four-Four Rhythms

For each of the following, start by using you thumb, then add in a forefinger if it feels comfortable, finally, try it with a plectrum*.

Hold a chord that you feel comfortable making, and when you get the feel change the chord after ever bar, or four beats.

Set the metronome to sixty beats per minute, then when you get the hang of the rhythm, increase it to eighty beats per minute.

Example One

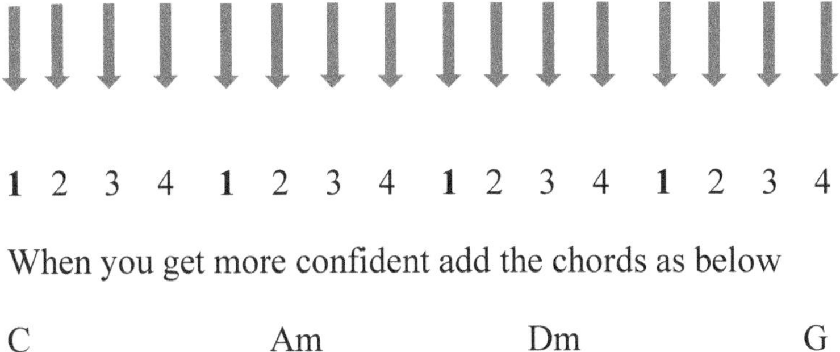

When you get more confident add the chords as below

C   Am   Dm   G

Example Two

This time you will strum twice as quickly, getting eight strokes in each four beats. Start with a down beat / strum and follow it with an upbeat. Once again, add the different chords when you have the hang of it. Don't forget to use your metronome to make sure you maintain a rhythm and keep time.

Example Three

Once you have these basics, then we can go for something very complicated. After you have mastered this and the chords we have shown you, you really will be able to call yourself a guitar player. Perhaps not yet an Eric Clapton, Jimi Hendrix or Paul Simon, but definitely someone who can bash out a beat, play the chords and make it sound good.

As before, start with the single chord and the slow speed, then build things up. Note the direction of the strokes.

Note that here the first 'stroke' of the third beat does not happen. The effect you are looking to achieve is **DUM   DEE DEE pause DEE DEE DEE DUM   DEE DEE pause DEE DEE DEE** etc.

A Tip for the Plectrum

It is best to start with a medium weight plectrum, as they are easiest to manipulate. Heavy ones can get caught on the strings, and lightweight ones can be harder to control. Hold the plectrum between your thumb and first finger, and curl the other fingers up into a loose fist. Hold the plectrum towards the top, so just over half is exposed to strike the strings. You do not want the strings to catch on your fingers.

Finally, remember when strumming that the movement comes from the wrist, not the whole arm. The great arm flashing helicopter rotors of Pete Townshend and other performers are for show, not effect. Just a small rotation of the wrist leads to controlled, pure strumming with a great sound.

Chapter Summary

In this chapter we have learned a little about strumming, the technique and some rhythms that can be played.

In the next chapter we will learn something a little more technical: reading tabs.

Chapter Four: Lesson Four - Reading Tabs

There are four basic ways to play the notes and chords, found in a piece of music, on the guitar. These are:

- Reading the Music
- Playing by Ear
- Reading Chord Names
- Playing by Tab

Reading Music

The guitar is unusual when it comes to instruments. First, compared to most, it is relatively easy to learn. There is none of the complex finger movements of the piano, breathing challenges of wind and brass instruments or judgement of tone and pitch associated with the likes of the violin and cello.

That means that players are often self-taught, from books such as this, or have picked it up from friends. Learning to read music is a very useful skill indeed, but it is time consuming and needs a lot of practice. It tends to be an element left out when learning the guitar without the benefit of formal tutorage.

However, there is a use in knowing where the various notes are located on the guitar. These are presented in the table below. Along the top are the fret positions, down the side are the strings to which the fret position is related and finally in the middle is the note played. The logical pattern will quickly become apparent. Remember that the following pairs of notes are the same:

A# and Bb, C# and Db, D# and Eb, F# and Gb, G# and Ab

Open	First	Second	Third	Fourth	Fifth	Sixth	Seventh	Eighth
E (first)	F	F#	G	G#	A	Bb	B	C
B (second)	C	C#	D	Eb	E	F	F#	G
G (third)	G#	A	Bb	B	C	C#	D	Eb
D (fourth)	Eb	E	F	F#	G	G#	A	Bb
A (fifth)	Bb	B	C	C#	D	Eb	E	F
E (sixth)	F	F#	G	G#	A	Bb	B	C

Playing by Ear

There are some natural musicians who can just hear a piece, and know how to play it and which chords or notes to use. Sadly, not many of us fit into that category.

117

Playing by Chords

This is the easiest way of playing. Here, the chords to play are written above the lyrics of the song. The only problem is that if you do not know the song, it can be very hard to play. Getting the placement of the actual chord changes is also very difficult. Simply placing the fingers in the exact place is a challenge. There are some songs using this method later in the book, to get players started.

Playing by Tab

This might seem complicated at first, but with a bit of time, can be a very helpful way of overcoming the difficulties listed above.

The tab is a horizontal box with six lines, each one equating to one of the guitar's strings. The lowest represents the low E string, next is the A string, the D string, G string, then one from the top is the B string, with the top line equating to the higher pitched E string.

Numbers printed on the strings relate to the fret that the string should be played on. A '0' means that the string should be played open.

Chords are a little more complicated, but still quick to learn. Here, numbers appear on all the strings.

Can you work out which chord the following tablature represents?

It is, of course, E major. Strings 1 (E), 2 (B) and 6 (E) are open, then the G string is played on the first fret, and strings 4 and 5, (D and A) are played on the second fret.

To help even more, tablature, or tabs, will usually feature the chord's name as well.

A little later we will learn a bit about finger picking. This is when the notes of the chord are played individually by the fingers of, for right handed players, the right hand. The proper name for this is an arpeggiated chord*.

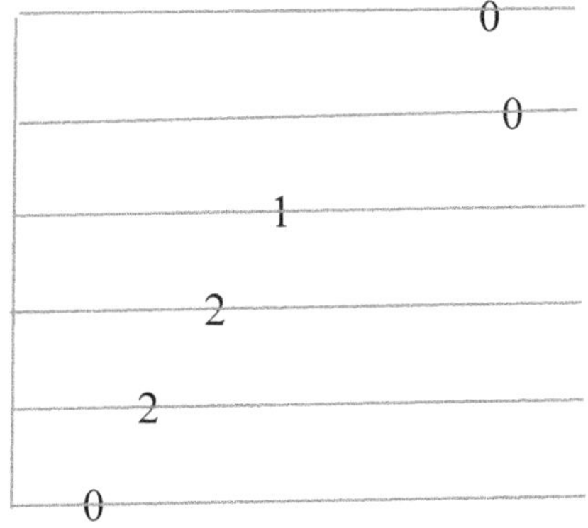

The arpeggiated E major chord will look like the diagram above.

Where a string should not be played, it is indicated by an X. There are numerous other signs in tablature, which can be investigated when a player is more competent with their instrument, but this is enough information for the first stages of playing, especially as this book aims to get players up and running, at the most basic level, within a day.

Chapter Summary

In this chapter we have learned four ways of playing the guitar. By chord, by ear, by music and by tab.

- Playing by chord is the most straightforward, but is a rough science.
- Tab and music are accurate, but trickier (especially by music).
- Playing by ear is an aptitude all musicians would like, but few possess.

In the next chapter we talk about barre chords, the method by which any chord can be played.

Chapter Five: Lesson Five - Barre Chords

In this chapter you will learn about how the barre can turn the basic chord shapes into any chord.

Creating the barre can be tiring at first, and strength needs to build up in the hand. It is easiest on an electric guitar, where the neck is slim and the strings are usually lightweight. The Spanish guitar is hardest because of the width of the neck and the bulkiness of the strings.

Below we can see how the basic E chord fingering turns into the chord of F when it is shifted down a fret, and the index finger makes a barre behind it.

F

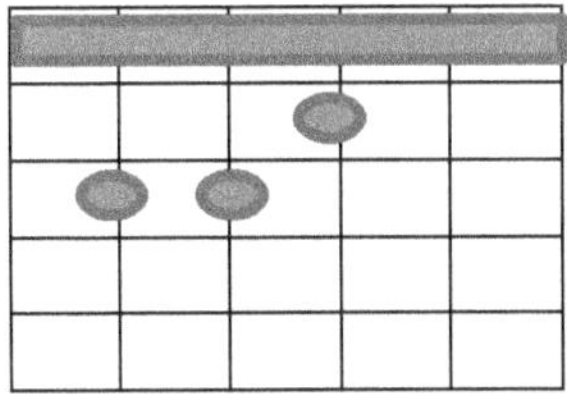

Here are some of the chords that we did not show earlier, with their barre in place

B Chords

B

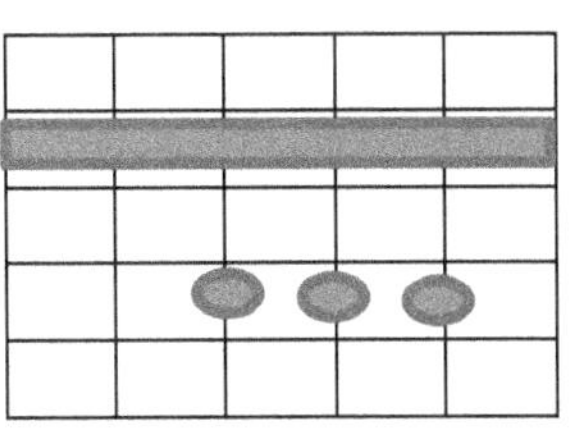

Bm

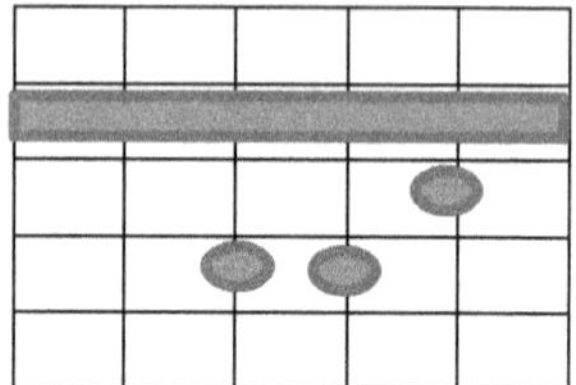

B7 (no low E strummed)

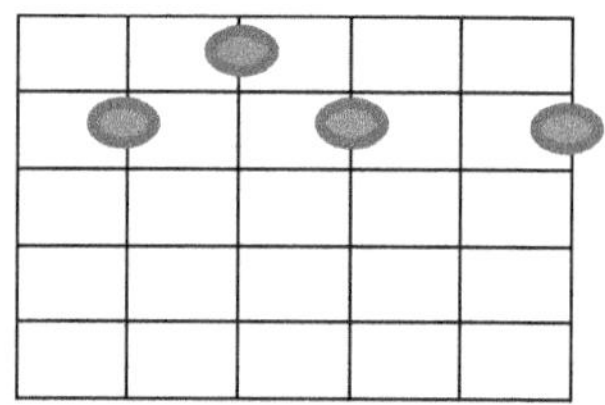

Bm7

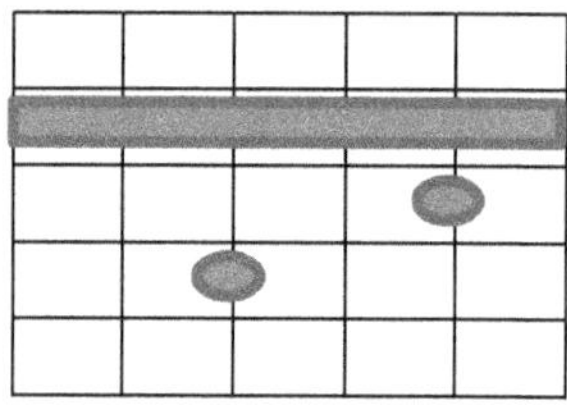

F Chords

Fm

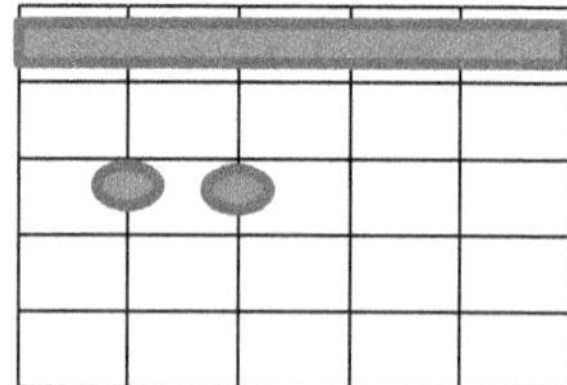

F7

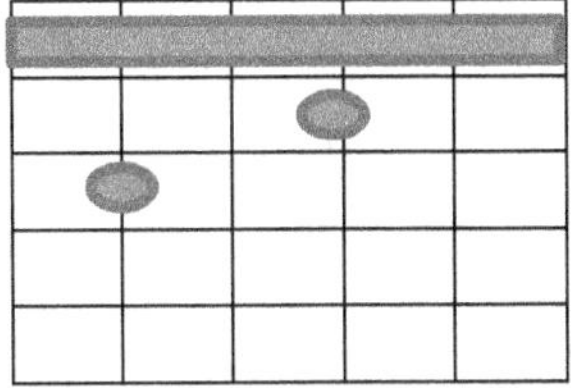

Fm7

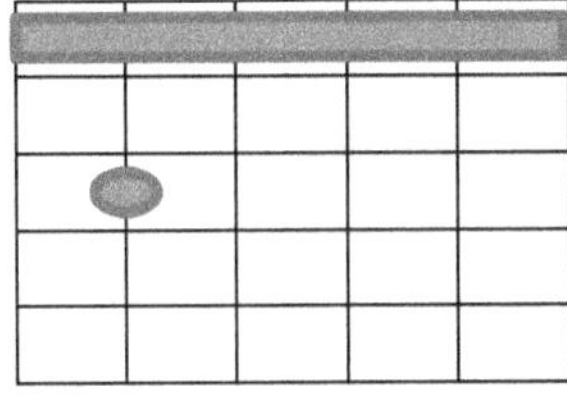

G Chords

Gm

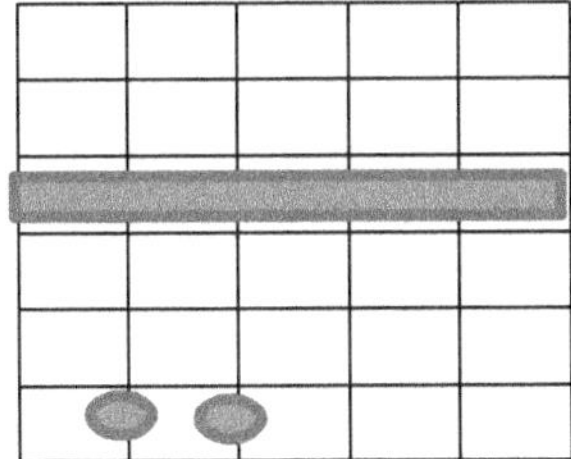

Gm7

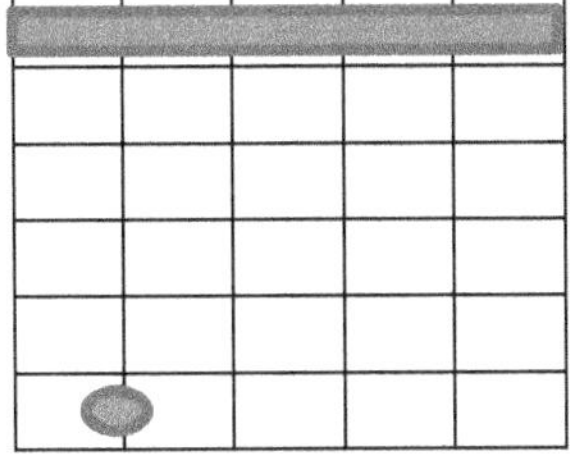

123

Sharps and Flats

Sharp and flat chords tend to be made using a barre. The most common chords here are F sharp (F#), C#, B flat (Bb) and Eb, although there are several more.

F#

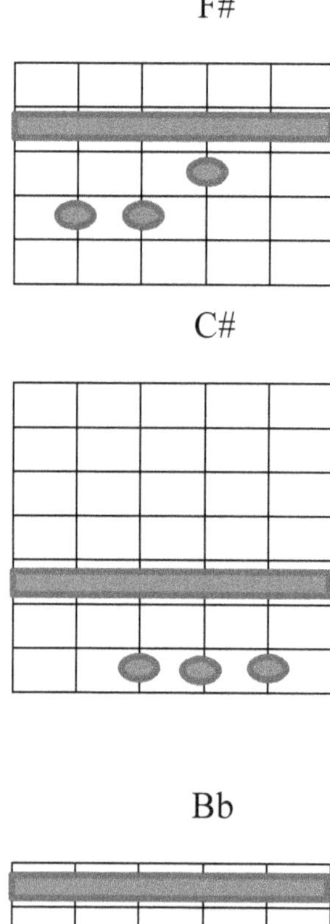

C#

Bb

Eb

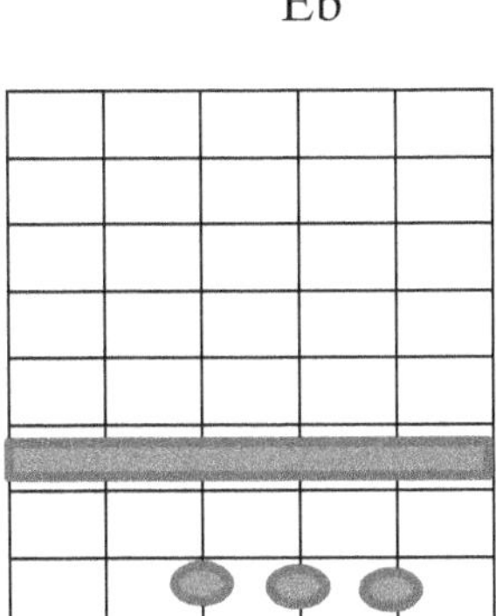

As many of you will have spotted, it is possible to play the same chord in many ways using a barre. This can make chord changes easier as players become more experienced. Although the chord is the same, the pitch and quality of sound will vary depending on where on the fretboard* the chord is played.

Chord Table

The table below shows how various chords are formed depending on where they are played on the fretboard. Chord shapes are listed across the top, and the fret on which the barre is held down the side.

In the middle is the chord that is formed. The pattern can be repeated for any cord shape, although these are the shapes that are usually to be found used with a barre.

	E	Em	Em7	A	Am	Am7
1st	F	Fm	Fm7	Bb	Bbm	Bbm7
2nd	F#	F#m	F#m7	B	Bm	Bm7
3rd	G	Gm	Gm7	C	Cm	Cm7
4th	Ab	G#m	G#m7	C#	C#m	C#m7
5th	A	Am	Am7	D	Dm	Dm7
6th	Bb	Bbm	Bbm7	Eb	Ebm	Ebm7
7th	B	Bm	Bm7	E	Em	Em7
8th	C	Cm	Cm7	F	Fm	Fm7

Chapter Summary

In this chapter we have looked at the barre.

- We have seen that the barre accompanied by the shapes of other chords can create new chords.

- Practising with a barre makes chord changes easier.

In the next chapter you will learn more about those essentials of instrument playing, scales.

Chapter Six: Lesson Six - Guitar Scales

Quite a short chapter this one, but a very important one. Scales are the notes that are contained within a particular key in music. Songs are written in keys, and by knowing the notes that are involved in that key, it is possible to play accompaniments and lead guitar to go with it.

A great way to warm up is to run through a couple of scales, it gets the fingers of both hands working, and over time the notes will become engrained in your head. You will then know, even if you are just reading the chords involved in a piece, the key in which it is based.

The tables below show the notes involved in all the major and minor keys. The numbers on the left indicate the place of that note in the scale, while the keys are across the top.

Major Keys

	A	Bb	B	C	Db	D	Eb	E	F	F#	G	Ab
1	A	Bb	B	C	Db	D	Eb	E	F	F#	G	Ab
2	B	C	Db	D	Eb	E	F	F#	G	G#	A	Bb
3	C#	D	Eb	E	F	F#	G	G#	A	Bb	B	C
4	D	Eb	E	F	F#	G	Ab	A	Bb	B	C	Db
5	E	F	F#	G	Ab	A	Bb	B	C	C#	D	Eb
6	F#	G	Ab	A	Bb	B	C	C#	D	D#	E	F
7	Ab	A	Bb	B	C	C#	D	D#	E	F	F#	G
8	A	Bb	B	C	Db	D	Eb	E	F	F#	G	Ab

Minor Keys (Harmonic Minors)

	A m	Bb m	B m	C m	C# m	D m	Eb m	E m	F m	F# m	G m	G# m
1	A	Bb	B	C	C#	D	Eb	E	F	F#	G	G#
2	B	C	C	D	D#	E	F	F#	G	G#	A	A
3	C	Db	D	Eb	E	F	Gb	G	Ab	A	Bb	B
4	D	Eb	E	f	F#	G	Ab	A	Bb	B	C	C#
5	E	F	F#	G	G#	A	Bb	B	C	C#	D	D#
6	F	Gb	G	Ab	A	Bb	C	C	Db	D	E	E
7	G#	A	Bb	B	C	C#	D	D#	E	F	F#	G
8	A	Bb	B	C	C#	D	Eb	E	F	F#	G	G#

There are many different types of minor scales, such as harmonic (which is printed), melodic and natural scales. However, the harmonic is fine for using at the level we are currently at.

One of the most common and popular scales for the guitar is the blues scale.

The blues scale in C includes the following notes:

C	Eb	F	Gb	G	**Bb**	C

In the key of D, it looks like this:

D	F	G	Ab	A	C	D

Finally, we will learn the classic series of notes that, once mastered, lead to the classic 12 bar blues themes that underpin so many songs.

In tab form, it looks like this:

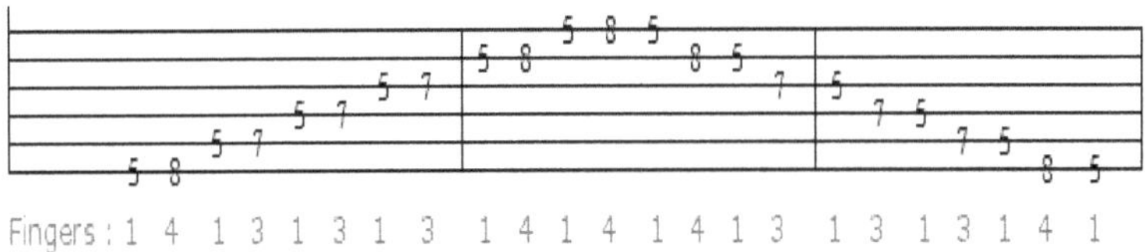

In notes, it is played as follows:

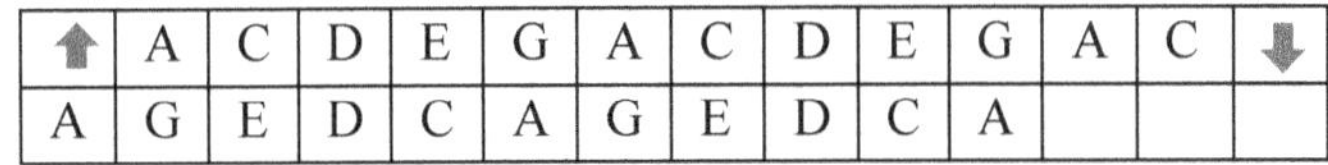

⬆	A	C	D	E	G	A	C	D	E	G	A	C	⬇
A	G	E	D	C	A	G	E	D	C	A			

Chapter Summary

Chapter six has introduced you to the concept of the musical scale. You have been given the notes involved in the different key signatures in which music is written.

In the next chapter you will learn more about plectrums or picks, and a little about finger picking.

Chapter Seven: Lesson Seven - Using a Plectrum and Finger Picking

As we saw earlier, there are many different weights of plectrum. It is best to start strumming with a middle weight one, and over time players will find the weight that suits them best, and which works for the kind of music they are playing. Heavy plectrums tend to be easier for picking notes if, for example, a combination of picking and strumming is required. Lightweight plectrums are handy for faster, smoother strumming. They are handy for electric guitars, where the sound is created electronically.

There are also thumb and finger picks which can be worn when picking notes. They can be tricky to use, catching on the strings, and a light action is needed. As a beginner, it is probably best to start picking using the fingers, rather than the picks shown below, but it is a matter of choice. A sharper sound is created with the picks.

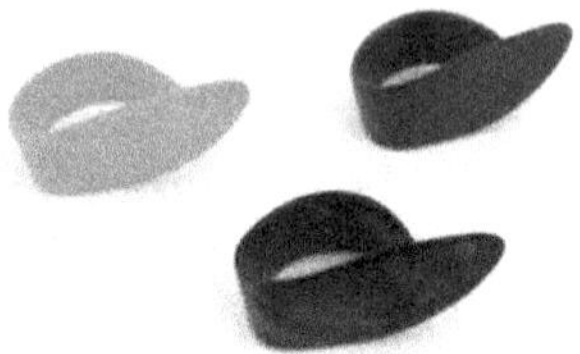

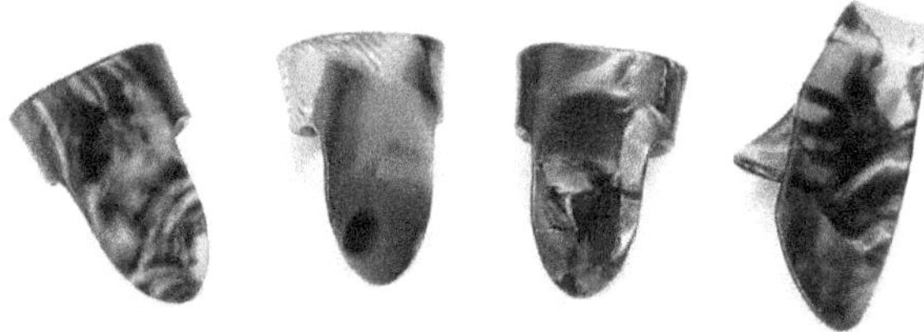

Whether picking or strumming, a different tone is created depending on where the action takes place. Playing over the sound hole (or pick up, with an electric guitar) creates the fullest, and loudest sound.

Move towards the bridge, and a harsher tone is produced. Unsurprisingly, playing closer to the neck makes for a softer, more mellifluous sound.

Finger Picking

Sometimes called finger style*, or plucking*, this is the method by which individual notes of a chord are played one after the other, often quite quickly. It is a style often associated with folk style music, and ballads.

Listen to Paul Simon playing the opening to the Simon and Garfunkel hit, The Boxer, to hear finger picking at its best.

Picking usually works as follows. The thumb plays any notes on the low E, A and D strings, while the first, second and third fingers pick notes from the G, B and E strings. Normally, the index finger will pluck the lowest string being played, usually the G string, with the middle finger next, usually the B string and the third finger used for the top E string. The little finger is not used, and many players place it under the sound hole on the body of the guitar to provide support and help the other fingers to remain in the correct place. The only time it would come into play is if there is a need to pluck five strings simultaneously.

Picking can be used with arpeggiated chords, and for playing pairs of notes together

An advantage of finger picking is that it turns the guitar into more than a percussive rhythm keeper. It allows for melodies to be interspersed with chords, and for the playing of harmonies (notes combined to produce a pleasing effect). Hammers* and pull offs* can also be incorporated into playing, as the guitarist becomes more competent. Tapping the body of the guitar to create a percussion effect is also easier than when working with a plectrum.

It is still possible to strum, using the thumb or first finger, but the sound created has a different quality to that created with a pick, and therefore it is not suitable for more upbeat rockier numbers.

Finger pickers need to keep their hands in good condition. The right hand always needs short finger nails for pressing the strings, and the same is true for the finger picker, unless they choose to use artificial picks. A nail too long will catch on the string, spoiling the effect being sought.

Another advantage with finger picking is that a greater variety of sound can be created. Generally, the volume will be lower, but varying the position of where the strings are plucked, and the force with which this happens, can alter the timbre*, to create mood and atmosphere in a song.

More flexibility is offered when playing, flamenco style strumming, plucking of multiple strings, arpeggios and such like all are easier to play with fingerpicking. However, the strings used should be nylon or light gauge steel, unless an artificial pick is attached to the fingers, to prevent nail and finger damage.

All the above makes it clear that finger picking lends itself to classical, solo guitar playing or playing as an accompaniment to voice or just perhaps one or two other instruments.

When finger picking is notarised in a piece of music, it will usually adopt the following notations:

Thumb = B

Index = I

Middle = M

Ring = A

Little = C or X or E

What's Next

As with everything else when learning the guitar, practice is all.

There are two simple finger picking exercises that can be practised to get the player into the swing.

For each, use the thumb for the E, A and D strings, the index finger for the G string, middle finger for the B string and third finger for the top E.

Use the chord progressions from earlier to practice. Set the metronome for 60 – it can get faster as you progress.

The first pattern is for 3/4 timing, the second for 4/4.

We will use the Dm, C, G, Dm progression in the example below. We will be playing two strings for each beat of the bar.

It goes something like this:

3/4 Example

The top row represents the chord, the second the finger playing and the third is the beat.

Dm						C						G						Dm					
T	I	M	A	M	I	T	I	M	A	M	I	T	I	M	A	M	I	T	I	M	A	M	I
1		2		3		1		2		3		1		2		3		1		2		3	

And so on…

4/4 Example

Dm								C								G							
T	I	M	A	M	I	T	I	T	I	M	A	M	I	T	I	T	I	M	A	M	I	T	I
1		2		3		4		1		2		3		4		1		2		3		4	

Chapter Summary

In this chapter we have learned a bit about finger picking, its uses and tools that can help.

- We know about how the notation is present
- We have undertaken some practice
- We know the kind of music with which it works best.

In the next chapter we will present some songs for you to play.

Chapter Eight: Some Songs to Play

Below are some songs along with their chords. They are well known, and if one is unfamiliar, they can be found easily on the internet. For legal reasons, we can only print songs that are out of copywrite, but there are hundreds of examples of popular music on the internet, plus countless books available from your local music stores.

Sing along with the songs, it will help you to 'feel' where the changes take place and keep you in time.

Happy Birthday

```
    A        E
Happy Birthday to you
    D     A
Happy Birthday to you
    A7       D
Happy Birthday dear Billy (please feel free to substitute a
name!)
    A    E   A
Happy Birthday to you.
```

Morning Has Broken

          C Dm G   F   C
Morning has broken, like the first morning
(C)   Em Am D7   D   G
Blackbird has spoken, like the first bird
C   F   C   Am D
Praise for the singing, praise for the morning
G   C F G7   C   F
Praise for the springing fresh from the world
[Interlude]
G E Am G C G7

            C Dm G   F   C
Sweet the rain's new fall, sunlit from heaven
(C)   Em Am D7   D   G
Like the first dewfall, on the first grass
C   F   C   Am D
Praise for the sweetness of the wet garden
G   C F G7   C   F
Sprung in completeness where his feet pass
[Interlude]
G E Am F# Bm G D A7/D D
        D Em A   G   D
Mine is the sunlight, mine is the morning
        F#m Bm   E7   A
Born of the one light, Eden saw play
D   G   D   Bm E
Praise with elation, praise every morning
A   D G A7   D
God's recreation of the new day

G A F# Bm G7 C F C

        C Dm G   F   C
Morning has broken, like the first morning
(C)   Em Am D7   D   G
Blackbird has spoken, like the first bird
C   F   C   Am   D
Praise for the singing, praise for the morning
G   C F G7   C   F
Praise for the springing fresh from the world
[Outro]
G E Am F# Bm G D A7/D D

She'll Be Coming Round the Mountain

G
She'll be coming 'round the mountain
    G
When she comes.
     G
She'll be coming 'round the mountain
    D7
When she comes.
     G
She'll be coming 'round the mountain,
     C
She'll be coming 'round the mountain,
     G   D7
She'll be coming 'round the mountain,
     G
When she comes.

[Verse 2]
     G
She'll be driving six white horses
     G
When she comes
     G
She'll be driving six white horses
    D7
When she comes
       G
She'll be driving six white horses
       C

She'll be driving six white horses
          G   D7
She'll be driving six white horses
       G
When she comes

[Verse 3]
        G
Oh, we'll all come out to meet her
        G
When she comes
        G
Oh, we'll all come out to meet her
        D7
When she comes
        G
Oh, we'll all come out to meet her
        C
Oh, we'll all come out to meet her
        G   D7
Oh, we'll all come out to meet her
        G
When she comes

[Verse 4]
        G
We will kill the old red rooster
        G
When she comes
        G
We will kill the old red rooster
        D7

When she comes
     G
We will kill the old red rooster
     C
We will kill the old red rooster
     G   D7
We will kill the old red rooster
     G
When she comes

[Verse 5]
     G
We'll all have chicken n' dumplin's
     G
When she comes
     G
We'll all have chicken n' dumplin's
     D7
When she comes
     G
We'll all have chicken n' dumplin's
     C
We'll all have chicken n' dumplin's
     G   D7
We'll all have chicken n' dumplin's
     G
When she comes

Swing Low, Sweet Chariot

C
I looked over Jordan,
  F   C
And what did I see,
                 G7
Comin' for to carry me home,
  C   F   C
A band of angels comin' after me,
       G7   C
Comin' for to carry me home.

      C   F C
Swing Low, sweet chariot,
                 G7
Comin' for to carry me home;
     C   F C
Swing low, sweet chariot,
C   G7   C
Comin' for to carry me home.

The Drunken Sailor

Em
What shall we do with the drunken sailor?
D
What shall we do with the drunken sailor?
Em
What shall we do with the drunken sailor?

[Chorus]

Em D   Em
Ear-ly in the morning
Em
Hooray, and up she rises
D
Hooray, and up she rises
Em
Hooray, and up she rises
Em D   Em
Ear-ly in the morning

[Verse]

Em
Put him in the long boat 'til he's sober
D
Put him in the long boat 'til he's sober
Em
Put him in the long boat 'til he's sober

[Chorus]

Em D   Em
Ear-ly in the morning
Em
Hooray, and up she rises
D
Hooray, and up she rises
Em
Hooray, and up she rises
Em D   Em
Ear-ly in the morning

[Verse]

Em
Pull out the plug and wet him all over
D
Pull out the plug and wet him all over
Em
Pull out the plug and wet him all over

[Chorus]

Em D   Em
Ear-ly in the morning
Em
Hooray, and up she rises
D
Hooray, and up she rises

Hooray, and up she rises

Em
Hooray, and up she rises
Em D   Em
Ear-ly in the morning

[Verse]

Em
Put him in the bilge and make him drink it
D
Put him in the bilge and make him drink it
Em
Put him in the bilge and make him drink it

[Chorus]

Em D   Em
Ear-ly in the morning
Em
Hooray, and up she rises
D
Hooray, and up she rises
Em
Hooray, and up she rises
Em D   Em
Ear-ly in the morning

[Verse]

Em
Put him in a leaky boat and make him bale her
D
Put him in a leaky boat and make him bale her
Em
Put him in a leaky boat and make him bale her

[Chorus]

Em D   Em
Ear-ly in the morning
Em
Hooray, and up she rises
D
Hooray, and up she rises
Em
Hooray, and up she rises
Em D   Em
Ear-ly in the morning

[Verse]

Em
Tie him to the scuppers with the hose pipe on him
D
Tie him to the scuppers with the hose pipe on him
Em
Tie him to the scuppers with the hose pipe on him

[Chorus]

Em D   Em
Ear-ly in the morning
Em
Hooray, and up she rises
D
Hooray, and up she rises
Em
Hooray, and up she rises
Em D   Em
Ear-ly in the morning

[Verse]

Em
Shave his belly with a rusty razor
D
Shave his belly with a rusty razor
Em
Shave his belly with a rusty razor

[Chorus]

Em D   Em
Ear-ly in the morning
Em
Hooray, and up she rises
D
Hooray, and up she rises

Em
Hooray, and up she rises
Em D   Em
Ear-ly in the morning

[Verse]

Em
Tie him to the topmast while she's yardarm under
D
Tie him to the topmast while she's yardarm under
Em
Tie him to the topmast while she's yardarm under

[Chorus]

Em D   Em
Ear-ly in the morning
Em
Hooray, and up she rises
D
Hooray, and up she rises
Em
Hooray, and up she rises
Em D   Em
Ear-ly in the morning

[Verse]

Em
Heave him by the leg in a runnin' bowline
D
Heave him by the leg in a runnin' bowline
Em
Heave him by the leg in a runnin' bowline

[Chorus]

Em D   Em
Ear-ly in the morning
Em
Hooray, and up she rises
D
Hooray, and up she rises
Em
Hooray, and up she rises
Em D   Em
Ear-ly in the morning

[Verse]

Em
Keel haul him 'til he's sober
D
Keel haul him 'til he's sober
Em
Keel haul him 'til he's sober

[Chorus]

Em D   Em
Ear-ly in the morning
Em
Hooray, and up she rises
D
Hooray, and up she rises
Em
Hooray, and up she rises
Em D   Em
Ear-ly in the morning

Greensleeves

```
Am    C
Alas my love,
  G    Em
you do me wrong,
  Am         E
to cast me off so discourteously,
  Am    C    G    Em
for I have loved you so long,
  Am    E7    Am
delighting in your company.
```

[Chorus]

```
C         G    Em
greensleeves was all my joy,
Am         E
greensleeves was my delight,
C         G    Em
greensleeves was my heart of gold,
  Am      E7  Am
and who but my lady greensleeves.
```

[Verse 2]

```
  Am    C       G    Em
Thy gown was of the grassy green,
    Am         E
Thy sleeves of satin hanging by,
```

     Am   C   G   Em
Which made thee be our harvest queen,
 Am   E7   Am
And yet thou wouldst not love me.

[Chorus]

C   G   Em
greensleeves was all my joy,
Am   E
greensleeves was my delight,
C   G   Em
greensleeves was my heart of gold,
  Am   E7 Am
and who but my lady greensleeves.

[Verse 3]

 Am   C   G   Em
Well, I will pray to God on high,
   Am   E
That thou constancy mayst see,
 Am   C   G   Em
And that yet once before I die,
Am   E7   Am
Thou will vouchsafe to love me.

Jingle Bells

C
Dashing through the snow
          F
In a one horse open sleigh
         G
O'er the fields we go
        C
Laughing all the way
C
Bells on bob tails ring
         F
Making spirits bright
F   G
What fun it is to laugh and sing
G   C
A sleighing song tonight

C
Oh, jingle bells, jingle bells
C
Jingle all the way
F   C
Oh, what fun it is to ride
G
In a one horse open sleigh
C
Jingle bells, jingle bells
C
Jingle all the way
F   C

Oh, what fun it is to ride
G   (F)   C
In a one horse open sleigh

Chapter Nine: Stringing and Tuning Your Guitar

Playing the guitar when it has new strings is always a treat. The beautiful sounds of the strings and the quality of the notes make it seem as though you are playing a new instrument. However, fitting the little blighters is not such fun.

Remember, classical or Spanish guitars have nylon or gut strings, other varieties take steel strings. Put steel strings on a Spanish guitar and the stresses will be too much, resulting in damage to the body and neck.

If you are not going to be playing the guitar for a while, loosen the tension on the strings, it helps to take the pressure off the guitar's frame.

Restringing a Guitar

Little intricacies around the bridge can vary from guitar to guitar, but the basics are below.

Step One

Turn the tuning peg, loosening each of the existing strings, until all are quiet slack.

Step Two

Starting with the Low E string, keep loosening until the string can be pushed through its hole. Then, pull it out from the bridge. This may involve untying a knot, pulling by the little nut on the end of the string, or removing a string holder from the bridge by pulling, it will depend on your guitar.

Step Three

Repeat step two with all the other strings, starting with the A string, then through D, G, B and finishing with E.

Step Four

Take the bottom E string, the lowest note (it will be the thickest string, in its own little pack). Push the end through the hole in the bridge, and pull tight. Secure the string with whatever means the old string was secured by. Slide the string through the hole in its tuning peg, making sure that you have it in the correct peg. This first string will go through the first hole in the head at the top of the guitar.

Step Five

Pull the string tight, then feedback about 4-6 cm to create some slack.

Step Six

At the head end, angle the string slightly upwards and turn the tuning peg to tighten it. When the string is taught enough, position it in its slot in the nut of the guitar. That is the small, slotted strip where the neck meets the head. Tighten further until the string is sufficiently tense to remain in place in the nut. Don't worry about tuning yet.

Step Seven

Repeat steps four, five and six with the other strings, starting with the A string, then the D, G, B and finally the top E.

Step Eight

If you have excessive amounts of string hanging loose at the neck end, get some cutters and trim the strings. Leave about 3-4 cm showing.

You now have a restringed guitar…one that is very out of tune.

Tuning the Guitar

Unless you have purchased expensive, pre-stressed strings, then your guitar will go out of tune very quickly. You will need to retune regularly for a week or so. You will find that the guitar stays in tune for longer and longer periods.

First Tune

Unless you are blessed with perfect pitch, you will need something to tune the guitar to. A piano, tuning fork or measuring device attached to the head will do help you with this. Just as easy is to go online and search for a free guitar tuner. These work perfectly well.

Tuning the Guitar to itself

Once the instrument has settled after its re-stringing. It is much quicker to tune it to itself. This can be done in two ways.

Note Method

The fifth fret on the string is the same note as the open string on the next. So, pressing and playing the fifth fret on the A string, gives the note D, which is the same as the open D string.

The only exception is from the G string to the B string. Here, the fourth fret needs to be played to get the same note, B, as the open string after it.

Tune the string while holding down the note and letting both it and the open note ring on. Although requiring a bit of contortion, this allows you to hear the notes blend together.

Harmonic* Method

Harmonics are played by placing the finger of the left hand lightly on the string directly over a fret marker. The string is plucked and the finger lifted simultaneously. A bell like ringing sound is created.

Listening to the harmonics is a great way to tune, as rather than judging pitch, you will hear the vibrations of the harmonics. They will synch together when the notes are the same.

You will need to play harmonics on the fifth fret of the lower string, and seventh fret of the higher string to get the effect required. Unfortunately, this method does not work with the G to B strings, although it does with all other combinations.

Hearing Method

If you play a chord slowly, or two notes an octave* apart (use the table of notes in the earlier chapter to find where the same notes can be found) those with a good ear can hear whether their guitar is in tune or not. This gets easier with experience.

Tuning a Twelve String Guitar

If re-stringing a normal guitar is tricky, that is nothing to a 12 string. Tuning, too, is a little different.

For normal pitch, the main six strings are tuned as normal, but between each of the low E, A, D and G a string is fitted and pitched to an octave above the main note. The top two strings, B and top E, have their partners as identical pitch to themselves.

So, starting from the lowest string, the tuning is:

E (as per normal guitar)

E (up an octave)

A

A (up an octave)

D

D (up an octave)

G

G (up an octave)

B

B (same note, NOT up an octave)

E

E (same note, NOT up an octave)

Hard work, but a great sound.

Chapter Ten: Other Information

Types of Guitars

The main types are:

- *Spanish guitar*, usually the smallest kind, with nylon or gut strings, and a soft but precise sound. Usually finger picked, but can be strummed, usually with the thumb or fingers.
- *Acoustic Guitar*, steel stringed and usually finger picked or strummed with a plectrum.
- *Electric Acoustic*, as above with the addition of an electronic pick up to allow it to be played through an amplifier.
- *Electric Guitar*, often with one or two pick-ups, usually strummed or played as lead guitar – see below.
- *Bass Guitar*, four stringed electric with different tuning. Notes are usually plucked.
- *Combo*, a guitar with two necks allowing bass and normal guitar to be played.
- *Hollow Bodies Guitars* – these are electric guitars where the sound is enhanced with a hollow body. See below for an example.

- *Twelve String,* a steel strung acoustic usually strummed.
- *Hawaiian,* a guitar really in name only, although the steel tube with which the notes are formed can be bought for other guitar types.
- *Four and A Half String,* yes, really! Some of the earliest instruments were four stringed, with an extra, open string attached from the bridge to half way along the neck.

Looking After Your Guitar

You can get a decent, second hand model for $10, or you can pay thousands. Whichever, a guitar is a precision instrument and deserves to be treated as such. It is worth investing in a case to protect from everyday life. A soft one is fine if the guitar is to be kept at home, a hard one if it is going to be moved around, or the toddler can get access to it.

A soft, lint free duster can give the guitar a once over after it is played, removing finger marks, and specialist cleaners can be used to make it sparkle.

When the guitar is not in use, store it in a dry room, out of direct sunlight, away from a radiator and in a moderate temperature. Properly looked after, a guitar will last for life. In fact, for generations.

Buying a Guitar

Some things better with age. Cheese, fine red wine, Jane Fonda…many musical instruments also fit into this category. The guitar is no different. As the wood matures and settles, so the sound improves in quality. Therefore, there is no real need to buy new when $50 at a second hand will get a decent and very usable model. Double that for a new one.

But whether buying new or second hand, try out the instrument. Check that its weight is comfortable, and it is the right size. Elvis Presley played on a ¾ size instrument through the early part of his career, but he was a little special. Basically, make sure the guitar feels right when you hold it.

Check for cracks anywhere – if you find one walk away; a guitar is an instrument designed to take the stresses of tight strings, if there is a fault, it won't last for long. Check that there is no bowing on the back, and that the neck is straight.

Surface damage such as light scratches won't matter if they have not damaged the wood but if there are buzzes when played and the cause is not obvious (such as too much overhanging string at the head) then look elsewhere.

Make sure that the bridge is secure and the tuning parts are all in good condition.

Playing Lead

The lead guitarist is the quarter back, the centre forward, the Ferrari, the Tom Cruise of the guitar world. In other words, the glamour player. Listen to Pink Floyd or Dire Straits or Eric Clapton and hear the astonishing lead guitar melodies and riffs that take the music to that ultimate destination. Of course, just as Mr Cruise needs his support players and the quarterback (his team mates), so the lead is nothing without his rhythm back up.

But if lead is what you want, then a number of skills need to be developed. Some musical knowledge is needed, as lead improvisations come from an understanding of the constituent parts of the chord structure and key signatures being played.

Competency with both hands is needed. The left often picks notes at the end of the neck close to the body, where the frets are narrower, and more precision is needed. At the same time, picking notes with a plectrum is harder than doing it with the fingers.

But, as always, practice makes perfect and that starring role comes to those who want it and work for it.

If it is for you, start by grasping the first position. This is where notes are played using the first four frets, with the index finger on string one, and so forth ending with the little finger on fret four. Once tunes, melodies, harmonies and riffs* can be picked from here, then you can move on to working further down the fret board.

Accessories

Here is a list of some helpful accessories. Not all of these are required, so we have listed a usefulness factor after each. 1/5 means you may not need this item whereas 5/5 means you should have that item for playing regularly.

- *Stand* - frame for holding the guitar when it is not being used. It will add protection to the guitar and help preserve its life.   4/5
- *Footstool* – a handy device for serious Spanish guitar players and beginners as they get the guitar position right. To be honest, though, a pile of books works as well.   1/5

- *Plectrums and Picks* – essentials, especially plectrums, for the acoustic and electric guitar player. 5/5 (plectrums) 2/5 (finger picks)
- *Tuning Paraphernalia* – necessary in the old days, when a tuning fork was the only way to get into tune if there was no piano in the house. Nowadays it is all available online. 3/5 (because an portable tuner is always handy)
- *Metronome* – a handy tool for the beginner. A good, old fashioned metronome does the job and looks great, but as with tuning equipment, a metronome can be found for free through an app or online. 3/5 (but only for its decorative qualities)
- *Guitar Cover* – it will prolong the life of your instrument. 5/5
- *Strap* – depends on the type of guitar. Classical or Spanish guitars rarely come with strap holders as they are meant to be played sitting down. But if you have an electric, then you look a bit silly playing while sitting, at least if there is an audience. 3/5
- *Amplifier* – in the old days, your amp could double as a nuclear fallout shelter, so big and sturdy was the speaker. Now, for $50, a tiny amp capable of filling a large hall with sound is readily available. Pay more, and all kinds of effects will come as well. 5/5 for electric guitars.
- *Effects Pedals* – as spectacular as it looks, stamping on pedals while sweat pours of your face staining the silver lycra and making the Bowie Make Up run, these are a bit, well, seventies. Just get a decent amp. 0/5

- *Music Stand* – from the mad to the sensible. A music stand will hold your music at the right level whether you stand or sit. Admittedly, a table also works, as does a chair and, if your eyesight is good enough, the floor. But, a music stands makes you look professional 2/5

Chapter Ten: Glossary – In Very Simplified Terms

Acoustic Guitar – Steel stringed and slightly larger than a classical guitar. Associated with folk music, some pop music. Ideal for strumming or picking.

Arpeggiated Chord – a chord where the individual notes are picked out one at a time.

Barre – Using the first finger to cover all six strings. This has the effect of allowing the basic chord shape to be played anywhere on the guitar neck. So, for example, the E shape creates the chord E when there is no barre. With a first fret barre, and the same shape after it, the chord moves up from an E to an F, one more and it becomes F#, next G, G#. A, A# (usually called Bb of B flat), C, C#, D, Eb (the same as D#) and then back to E.

Bass Guitar – Not covered in this book, but a four-stringed variety, with each string of a lower pitch than in the six-string variety, usually electric.

Chord – a combination of notes played together.

Classical Guitar – sometimes called Spanish Guitar, these are slightly smaller than other types usually. They are nylon stringed and can be used for classical music, finger picking and, sometimes, strumming.

Clef – the symbol in music which gives an indication of pitch. The guitar uses the treble clef, but never the bass clef. The clef appears at the beginning of a sheet of music.

Electric Guitar – Played through an amp. The easy action of electric guitars makes them comfortable to play. Ideal for lead or rhythm work. Less good for finger picking.

Finger Picking – playing notes individually, occasionally in pairs, with the thumb and fingers of the right (for right handed guitarists) hand.

Finger Style – see Finger Picking

Fret – The zones marked on the neck of the guitar. Each fret is marked by a narrow strip which runs perpendicular to and below the strings.

Fretboard – the frets on the neck of the guitar.

Hammer – playing a note by banging the left hand onto the string at the correct fret for the note.

Harmonics – bell like sounds played by placing the finger of the left hand lightly on the string directly above the fret marker. As the string is plucked, the finger lifts. A good place to practice is on the 12th fret for each string, where harmonics are easy to play.

Hawaiian Guitar – often played flat, they are tuned by using a hollow tube, which creates a unique, smooth and tropical sound. It is possible to buy the tubes and use them on other kinds of guitars.

Jamming, or Jam Session – informal playing with others.

Key – music is written in a 'key' – it tells you the combination of 'rules' that make the piece sound 'right'. The guitar is tuned to the key of E minor 7 with a suspension. There, that makes a lot of sense. It is possible to tune a guitar to a different key, but there are risks; the strings have a limit to which they can be stretched, and will snap if over tightened. Equally, if too slack, they will 'buzz' when played. It is best to stick in the natural key, which is changed through utilizing the frets and different chord placements.

Major Chords – those that sound full and complete.

Minor Chords – those chords that have a kind of questioning quality to them.

Notes – a note is the individual note that is made by playing a string. The notes change when the finger pushes down a string in a fret.

Octave – the group of eight notes between the same notes at different pitches. So, from C to C is an octave where D, E, F, G, A and B all fit between the two C notes.

Open String – this is the string when played with no notes pressed down on the frets. Starting from the string at the TOP of the guitar, the thickest string (which, confusingly, is the lowest note) they are E A D G B E.

Pick – sometimes called a plectrum, this is a triangular piece of thin plastic that comes in different widths – thin or light, medium and thick or heavy. It is used to strike the strings in an upwards or downward motion when strumming.

Plectrum – sometimes called a pick, this is a triangular piece of thin plastic that comes in different widths – thin or light, medium and thick or heavy. It is used to strike the strings in an upwards or downward motion when strumming.

Plucking – the action by which a note or notes are played by the right hand pulling the strings with a plucking action.

Pull off – a note played by the finger of the left hand pulling away from the string with a sharp, plucking action.

Riff – a repeated pattern of notes or chords.

Seventh Chords – a chord with an extra note.

Spanish Guitar - sometimes called Classical Guitar, these are slightly smaller than other types usually. They are nylon stringed and can be used for classical music, finger picking and, sometimes, strumming.

Strumming – the action of striking down the strings either with the thumb or plectrum (occasionally the first finger) when playing a chord.

Timbre – the musical quality of the sound created, often connected to mood and atmosphere.

Tuning or Tuned - these are the individual notes of the open strings. When played open (see above) they produce the following notes (see above). Starting from the string at the TOP of the guitar, the thickest string (which, confusingly, is the lowest note) they are E A D G B E.

Twelve String Guitars – as it suggests, twelve strings with clever tuning, creates a very full sound when strummed. Often used for country or folk type music.

Final Words

You have now reached the end of this introduction to the guitar. You could well be an expert player, about to organize your first gig in front of 1000 people at the local concert hall.

Much more likely is that practice, practice and more practice is what is needed next.

But competence will come quickly, given a bit of time. Twenty minutes a day will help you see rapid improvements in your playing and the acquisition of more and more skills.

Guitar playing is common, so it is easy to find advice from friends or the world wide web when you hit a problem. And that is a part of the joy of playing a guitar, or indeed any musical instrument.

You become a part of a community; a non-competitive, supportive and interesting one. There is enormous pleasure in playing your guitar by yourself, but even more by joining with others in a band, or just a friendly jam session* can be a lot of fun.

Make that your next step and now you are on the road to becoming a musician!

HOW TO PLAY
UKULELE
IN 1 DAY
The Only 7 Exercises You Need to
Learn Ukulele Chords, Ukulele Tabs
and Fingerstyle Ukulele Today
PRESTON HOFFMAN

BOOK 3

HOW TO PLAY UKULELE: IN 1 DAY

The Only 7 Exercises You Need to Learn Ukulele Chords, Ukulele Tabs and Fingerstyle Ukulele Today

Preston Hoffman

Table of Contents

Introduction

Welcome to '*How to Play Ukulele In 1 Day - The Only 7 Exercises You Need to Learn Ukulele Chords, Ukulele Tabs and Fingerstyle Ukulele Today*'! Thank you for purchasing my book. And congratulations! You have just taken the first step in learning how to play the ukulele in one day.

Whether you are learning to read music for the first time or are already a pro musician, this book will provide a collection of useful tips in seven easy-to-follow exercises that will get you playing the ukulele in one day.

The seven exercises cover the basic essentials of ukulele playing from how to buy your first ukulele and read chords to learning to fingerpick and strum your favourite songs.

I've been a musician for many years, playing all kinds of instruments from the guitar and piano to the drum and other percussion instruments. However, I've always had a soft spot for the ukulele. I love its cheerful sound and the diversity of music you can produce with it. When I first started playing it, I spent days of trial and error to get everything right. It wasn't easy, and I would have loved a guide on how to play. That's why I decided to gather my experience and research to present a comprehensive guide to playing the ukulele for anyone starting out.

It's an incredible instrument and it is, in fact, not that difficult to play. That's why I created seven easy steps to learn the ukulele in one day, so you can get the same amount of joy that I get playing it.

Enjoy the book! I hope you get as much pleasure out of reading it as I did writing and researching it.

Chapter One: Buying Your Ukulele

In this chapter, we will look at the main points you should consider before buying your ukulele.

Once you decide to start playing the ukulele, it's important that you invest in a good instrument that will produce a good sound and will last a long time. The first step is knowing your different ukuleles. Here are some points you should know.

➢ Most of the basic music shops will sell the Mahalo. They are a cheap and cheerful type of ukulele and come in every colour imaginable. While they tend to be popular in schools and for beginner ukulele players, they are not the best quality. If you really want to learn the ukulele, it's best to upgrade to something a bit better.

➢ A good quality ukulele is the Kala which isn't too expensive and produces a much better, clearer sound than the Mahalo. See if your local music retailer has Kalas in stock and test out a couple there. Alternatively, you can search online for a decent ukulele. Make sure you search on reputable music retailer websites to get the best quality ukulele you can and ask musicians that you know or even on online forums to get some recommendations for suppliers.

> However, there is more to the ukulele than buying the right brand and type. Another important factor is the strings as these are responsible for producing a good – or bad – sound. Good quality strings are not that expensive and are worth paying extra to ensure your ukulele is in the best quality possible. So, how can you be sure you are getting the best type of strings? Aquila is an excellent brand and will produce a nice, crisp sound. It's best to avoid the ukuleles with plastic-looking strings as these not only can break easily but they tend to produce a poor-quality sound.

> There are four sizes of ukulele. These are the soprano, concert, tenor, and baritone. The soprano can be considered the traditional ukulele with its classic ukulele sound and its small size of 20 inches. The next size up is the concert ukulele at 23 inches and is a little bit easier to handle than the soprano. A little bigger at 26 inches with a deeper sound is the tenor and is popular among professional ukulele players. Finally, there is the baritone which is the largest ukulele at 30 inches. This last type is probably the least popular among ukulele players who tend to be drawn towards the small size of the ukulele and, as a result, prefer to use smaller types.

Chapter Summary

In this chapter, you learned some tips on what to look out for when buying your first ukulele and some of the differences between the different types.

• When buying a ukulele, it's best to try and get the highest quality possible to make sure your instrument will last a long time and produce a quality sound.

• There are four different common types of ukulele. The soprano is the smallest and the type most associated with the ukulele. The baritone is the largest and the least popular due to its size.

In the next chapter, we will move onto the first lesson on how to learn the ukulele in one day. The first lesson will look at the different parts of the ukulele and how to hold it.

Chapter Two: Lesson One: The Parts of the Ukulele and How to Hold It

In order to learn how to play the ukulele, you first need to know the main parts of the instrument and how to hold it. In this chapter, we will be looking at the basics to get you started.

Why do I Need to Know the Parts of the Ukulele?

You may be keen to dive straight in and start playing, but first you need to learn the names of the parts. Why? Because this will allow you to tune, restring, and essentially take care of ukulele better. This is essential to produce a good quality sound and to make your instrument last longer.

Let's get familiar with the ukulele. Below is a picture of a ukulele.

It is made up of several parts that are essential for making it work and play music. A the very top, we have two important parts – the headstock and the tuners.

Headstock and Tuners

The headstock is also known as the head and is at the top of the ukulele. It needs to be strong to withstand the tension between the tuners and the strings, so it's often made of wood. The head on cheaper ukuleles will probably be made of plastic. The main role of the headstock is to hold the tuners.

The tuners have one of the most important jobs on the ukulele as they are responsible for tuning the strings. Although their most common name is tuners, they are sometimes known as machine heads, tuning pegs, tuning keys, tuning heads, or pegs. Each ukulele has four tuners and, as they are so important, let's look at them in more detail.

The direction that the tuners point in depends entirely on what ukulele you have. Some may point to the side whereas others may point backwards. It doesn't really matter which direction they point to, it's just something to be aware of. The strings of the ukulele are threaded through each tuner. The tuner, depending on the way it is turned, will either tighten the string or loosen it and this is what affects the sound. On the older ukuleles, the tuners depend on friction to turn it although this is an old-fashioned method nowadays. Modern ukuleles have geared tuners which are far easier to turn and if you buy a ukulele now, it's more than likely to have this type of tuner.

The first rule of tuning your ukulele is to gently unwind the tuner first before winding back up to get the right note. This prevents the string from over-stretching and helps avoid the string breaking in the long run. If your strings are made of metal, this rule is especially important.

Nut

Like the nut of the guitar, the nut of the ukulele is the area between the headstock and fretboard (the fretboard we will look at next) that holds the strings. It is a little ridge with small notches where the strings rest on. It helps to keep the strings in place and evenly spaced out. It also keeps the strings lifted off the board below which is essential for when you want to play the strings by pressing down on them.

Fretboard

The neck of the ukulele is what connects the headstock to the body of the instrument. The surface of the neck at the front is known as the fretboard and is the part beneath the strings. When buying an ukulele, you'll probably notice that a lot of the fretboards are black or dark brown. This is purely for aesthetic reasons and originates from when they used to be made of dark-coloured woods such as ebony.

Frets

Take a look at the fretboard and you will see the strips across it. These little bars ae known as frets. They are lifted off the surface to create a little bump and they get closer together as they get nearer to the sound hole.

Fret Markers

If you have played the guitar before, you may have noticed fret markers as well. These are the white indicators – or dots – that are placed on the fretboard. You may see other shapes or colours, but they are usually white and circular. They are useful to help you move up and down the fretboard and find certain notes.

Neck

If you remember, the fretboard is the surface of the neck and the neck is what supports the fretboard. To facilitate playing, the neck is curved and is usually made of wood to keep it strong and supported. It is directly connected to the head of the ukulele.

Body

The main part of the ukulele is called the body. The shape and size of the body influences the tone as when the strings vibrate, the body amplifies this sound. Ukuleles can have several different shapes and sizes depending on whether it is a more classic or modern type.

The Sound Hole

Like the guitar, the ukulele has a sound hole which, as the name lets on, helps amplify the sound. The sound played will be the loudest over the sound hole whereas higher up the fretboard will have the quietest sounds.

Bridge

The bridge is where the strings are attached, and it is found just under the sound hole. There are two types of bridges. First there is the tie-bar where the strings are threaded through and tied to the bridge. The other is a standard bridge where the string is threaded through a notch at the end of the bridge.

Saddle

The saddle is basically like the nut but at the opposite end of the board. Its role is to lift the strings off the fretboard and works with the nut to keep the strings in place and evenly spread out.

Strings

As we looked at before, it's important to choose your strings carefully. The choice of strings varies depending on the ukulele. For example, on concert and soprano ukuleles, the strings are quite often made of nylon. Other types of ukuleles may have a hybrid of nylon and metal. Some may have just metal strings which tend to produce a full-sounding tone.

Now you know all the parts of the ukulele. The next important part is learning how to hold it. Don't worry, it's pretty easy but you need to get it right from the start as this is what will help you master playing the ukulele in one day. As a note, the instructions below are for right-handed players. If you are left-handed, simply switch it the other way around.

How to Hold the Ukulele

First, prop the body of the ukulele against your chest with the neck supported by your left hand and your right forearm across the body with your strumming finger within easy reach of the strings. If it's a big ukulele, it's totally fine to rest it on one leg whilst your sitting to take the weight off your arms and to stop it from falling.

Your left hand will rest near the near top of the ukulele and keep your thumb behind the neck. It's a good idea to keep your nails short on your fretting hand – that's your left, your right is your strumming hand – as it makes sure that you play with the pad of your finger. Feeling comfortable is key and it may take a little while to get used to holding it in a way that feels natural. Don't worry – this will come.

Chapter Summary

In this chapter, we looked at the basics of the ukulele which are essential to know to get you off to the right start.

- You learnt the different parts of the ukulele including the tuners, the strings, the fretboard, and the bridge.

- You also learnt the best way of holding the ukulele to make sure you stay comfortable and are handling it in the best way to produce the best sound.

In the next chapter, we will look at the chords you should know. This will be the first step to learning how to play.

Chapter Three: Lesson Two: The Chords of The Ukulele

In this chapter, we will look at the chords. They are pretty easy to learn, and will you get you started playing straight away.

As we saw in the last chapter, you hold the neck of the ukulele in your left hand – this is assuming you play right-handed – and you strum with your right hand. In this case, it is your left hand that will form the chords.

To get the chords right, the first thing to know is that the ukulele has four chords. The chord sheets for the ukulele – also known as the Uke chord charts – have four lines, with each line representing one of the four strings.

The order of the chart starts with G, then to C, then to E, and finally to A with G at the left and A on the right. Try to remember them with an acronym, such as, Go Camping Every April, or whatever works best for you!

There are also major chords and minor chords.

> Major chords – make a definite, complete sound

> Minor chords – the sound is softer and almost a little moody.

With these four strings known as G, C, E, and A, you can create several different chords. When reading the chord sheets, there are two things to pay attention to. These are the dots at the top of the chart and the dots on the lines. The white dots at the top of the chart means that those strings don't need to be touched. This is known as an open string and you don't need to do anything about them. The black dot on the vertical line indicates which string you need to play and where, by showing if you should play the G, C, E, or A string and on which fret.

As you can see in the image below, to play this note, you would ignore G, C, and E and just play the A string. You would need to hold it down on the first fret, as the black dot shows. If the black dot was further down, for example by the line marked '3', then you would play string A on the third fret. And that's it! It's that simple to read the chord chart.

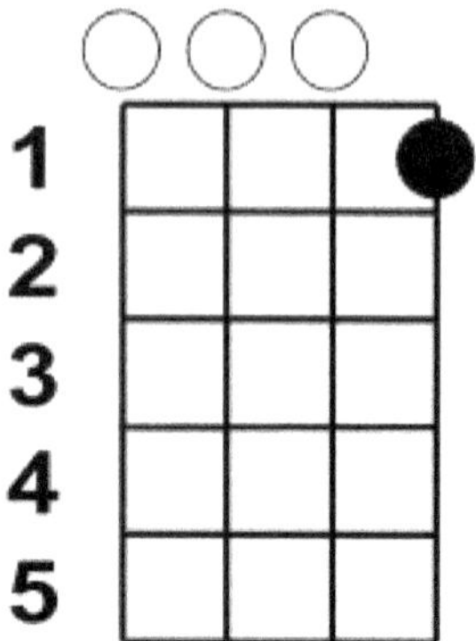

Let's begin with the first and easiest set of chords – the C chords.

C Chords

There are a few types of C chords – the C Major (C), C minor (Cm), and C7. These are the easiest set to play.

The C Major

To create the C major chord, you need to ignore the G, C, and E string and just hold down – or fret – the A string. The black dot for the C chord will always be on the third fret. So, to play the C chord, you need to fret the A string on the third fret.

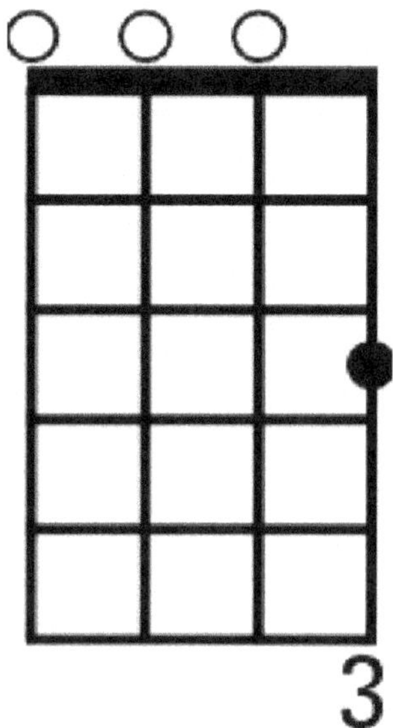

The C Minor

For the C minor, you need to hold down three strings – C, E and A – also on the third fret.

The C7 Chord

For the C7, you need to hold down the A string on the first fret.

The next set of chords we will look at are the A chords. Again, there is A major (A), A minor (Am), and A7.

The A Chords

The A Major

To play the A major, hold the G string on the second fret and the C string on the first fret.

A Minor Chord

Hold the G string on the second fret.

A7 Chord

Hold the C string on the first fret.

The next sets of chords we'll learn are the F, D, and G chords.

F Major Chord (F)

This time, to create the F major, you need to use two fingers. What you will do is ignore the C and A strings and just use the G and E strings. You need to hold down the E string on the first fret and the G string on the second fret. And that's it!

Tip: Using your left hand, place your index finger on the E string and your middle finger on the G string.

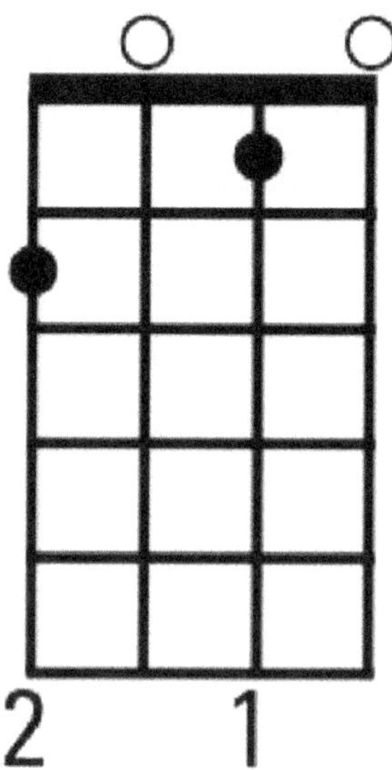

F Minor Chord (Fm)

You need to hold down the G string and the E string on the first fret, and the A string on the third fret.

D Major Chord (D)

You need to hold the G, C, and E string on the second fret.

D Minor Chord (Dm)

Hold down the G and C string on the second fret and the E string on the first fret.

G Major Chord (G)

Hold the C and A string on the second fret and the E string on the third fret.

These are all the most important chords you need to learn in the beginning and they should be easy to learn if you keep alternating between the chords and testing them out until they feel natural. But let's continue by looking at some of the other, slightly trickier chords.

B Chord

The B chord is not used that often in songs but it's worth knowing anyway. It has a complex feature known as the barre chord. The barre chord is when you need to play more than one string at the same time using the same finger.

To play the B chord, hold the G string on the fourth fret, the C string on the third fret, and finally, use your index finger to hold the E and A string together on the second fret. It takes practice but don't worry too much about it for now. You can come back to this chord later.

The B flat chord (Bb) is more common, especially in folk songs. It also has a barre chord.

B Flat

Hold the G string on the third fret, the C string on the second fret, and then you need to play a barre chord on the E and A string on the first fret.

It can be a bit tricky to hold all those strings at once in the beginning, so a good tip is to first master the G7 chord which is similar but a bit easier.

G7 Chord

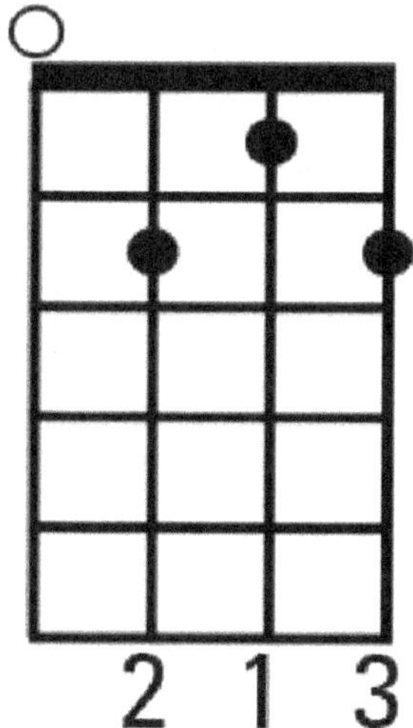

Hold the C chord on the second fret and make a barre chord on the E and A string on the first fret.

Next up is the important E chord. It's a bit more difficult as your fingers will need to stretch a lot which may feel strange in the beginning.

The E Chord

Hold the G string on the first fret, the C string on the fourth fret, and the A string on the second fret.

There is another E chord that you may see. It involves a barre chord on the G, C, and E strings on the fourth fret and holding down the A string on the second fret. Whichever one you choose, learning the E chord is important as it's present in a lot of songs.

Let's look at the other minor chords. These are a little complicated and don't expect to learn them overnight. However, it's fun to test them out anyway for now and learn to master them another day.

B Minor Chord (Bm)

This requires a barre chord on the C, E, and A string on the second fret and holding down the G string on the fourth fret.

E Minor Chord (Em)

Hold the C string on the fourth fret, the E string on the third fret, and the A string on the second fret.

G Minor Chord (Gm)

Hold the C string on the second fret, the E string on the third fret, and the A string on the first fret.

Finally, we have the 7 chords. These are commonly used in blues and jazz and can really add some groove to your music.

B7 Chord

This one is tricky and it's best to know about it now and practice later. You need to use a barre chord on the G, E, and A strings on the second fret and place your finger on the C string on the third fret.

D7 Chord

This one is also a little tricky. Use a barre chord on the G, C and E strings on the second fret and hold the A string on the third fret.

E7 Chord

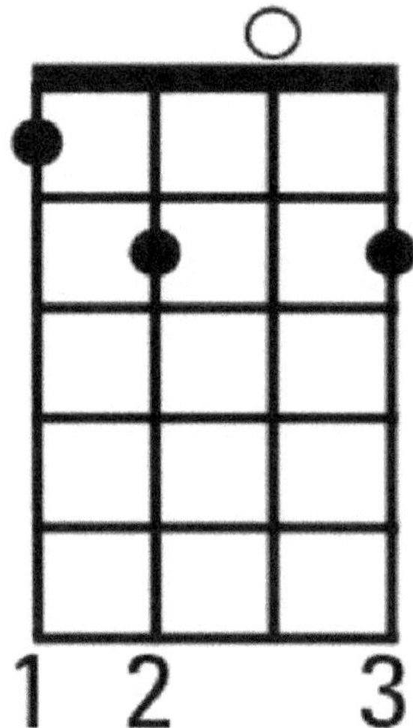

Hold the G string on the first fret, the C string on the second fret, and the A string on the second fret.

F7 Chord

Hold the G string on the second fret, the C string on the third fret, and the E string on the first fret. This is a but tricky in the beginning as it feels your fingers are all over the place! But it will eventually feel more natural.

These are all the chords you need to know in the beginning. Focus on learning the major chords and some of the minors. The chords you can leave for another day at the beginning, but they are worth learning to help you advance onto playing more varied songs quicker.

Chapter Summary

In this chapter, we learned about the different chords of the ukulele.

- The ukulele has four strings – G, C, E, and A.

- The main chords we looked at were the major, the minor, and the 7 chords. Some are easier – such as the C and A chords – than others – such as the E and 7 chords.

- It's worth spending some time practicing each chord individually before trying to transition between the chords. Learn the main chords though and you are good to start playing a wide range of different songs.

In the next chapter, we will learn more about transitioning between chords and chord progression.

Chapter Four: Lesson Three: Chord Transitioning and Chord Progression

In this chapter, we will look at chord transitioning – which is basically just moving from one chord to the next – and chord progression.

The first thing you need to do is to practice memorising the chords from the previous chapter. Don't worry if it doesn't happen overnight – remembering chords can take some time to commit to memory and it is totally fine to keep the chord charts open in front of you. It's better to make sure you are learning everything correctly from the beginning and getting used to where your fingers must go.

Once the chords become more natural, you can start transitioning between the chords.

Chord Transitioning

As mentioned before, chord transitioning is just moving between chords to create a song. Take it slow and steady in the beginning and in time, the flow and pace will quicken.

The easiest step to learning transitioning between the chords is moving between the G chord and the C chord.

To move between them, start with the G chord and place your fingers in the appropriate position. Your ring finger will be on the E string on the third fret. This will then need to be moved over to the A string, also on the third fret. Once it's there, lift the other fingers off the other strings and you are now on the C chord. Practice again a few times before trying to strum each note. It will become smoother and easier with time. That's all it takes to move between the G and C chord.

Next, we will move from the G chord to the F chord.

Put your fingers in the position of a G chord. Then move the index finger to the E string on the first fret and your middle finger to the G string on the second fret. Take the other finger off the other string as you don't need it for the F chord. And that's it!

Keep practising pairs like this to get used to moving between chords. How do you know which are the best chords to practice together though? This is where chord progression can help.

Chord Progression

Chord progression basically shows you the order of chords you need to play. Some chord charts show the chords as letters as we have seen already whereas others show the chords as roman numerals. To keep things simple, we will look at the chords as letters for now.

Music that sounds pleasant to the ear is just a combination of great sounding chords. If you have some experience already playing other musical instruments, you will know that some notes just sound better with some than others. The notes A minor, C major, D minor, and A7 sound nice together, as do A major, D major, and E7. These are some that you can practice together and try making your own tunes.

Here are some easy progressions to start with that will not only get you starting to play some basic songs, but will help you learn the feel of making transitions between chords.

C – F -G

These three chords can be played repeatedly in sequence in major.

Next up is C – Am – F – G

A little more challenging but great practice for getting your fingers used to the movements of the playing the ukulele.

Then try D – G – D -A7

Here are some more easy sequences to practice with:

Am – Dm – Am – E7

Here's one you may recognise from pop tunes.

Dm – A7 – Dm – Gm – A7 – Dm – A7 – Dm

Remember how the minor notes are often softer and quite moody? The sequence above is known as one of the saddest sequences of chords to play on the ukulele. It is used in the song Back to Black by Amy Winehouse, among other songs.

By using these chord progressions, it will help you to get used to changing between chords and start playing some basic tunes. It's the first step towards getting the natural beat of the chords, listening to what sounds good, and becoming more natural with playing.

Chapter Summary

In this chapter, we looked at how to transition between certain chords and how to practice using chord progression.

- An easy beginning is transitioning between the G and C chord then building up from there.

- Some chords naturally sound better together than others and you can make sequences of chords to make a tune. Chord progression is basically the order that you play the chords in. It is good to practice simple sequences in the beginning to get used to changing between chords and to have fun playing your first tunes.

In the next chapter, we will look at how to strum the ukulele.

Chapter Five: Lesson Four: How to Strum the Ukulele

In this chapter, we will look at the art of strumming the ukulele.

There is more to strumming than simply scraping your fingers across the strings over the sound hole. In fact, there is a lot more to it. Luckily, it is not that difficult to learn.

The basic technique is to use your index finger of your right hand with the fingernail facing down. What you are aiming for is to hit the string with your nail as you strum down. When you strum up, you will use the tip of your finger. So, strum down with your nail and strum up with the fleshy tip. It's natural in the beginning to use your whole hand to strum yet you should try just using your wrist to create the movements. This will make sure you don't tire out too quickly.

So now you have the basic technique of strumming, the where to strum part is pretty important too. If you strum too close to the bridge at the bottom, the sound won't be as good and comes out a bit muffled. The best spot can vary from ukulele to ukulele and it takes practice to know what sounds best. However, the best place is usually near to where the neck and the body meet.

To practice this technique, just strum up and down and get used to the rhythm. A great idea for practicing is to put on your favourite music and listen out for the beat. Once you catch it, try moving your hand up and down to match the pace, focusing on keeping the technique right.

Learning to strum shouldn't take too long at all so you will be well on your way to learning to play the ukulele at a strong beginner's level in one day.

Building Your Strumming Skills

The foundations of strumming are the simple up and down technique. Once you have nailed that, you can start experimenting with other tricks and tweaks. For example, you don't always need to just go up and down. You can skip a pattern so that instead of going down-up-down, you try down-up-up by not hitting the strings when you flick your wrist downwards. This helps build up different patterns and rhythms, creating a variety of sounds and beats to allow you to make your own unique music.

Let's look at some other ways you can jazz up your strumming skills.

➢ You can try doing the swing or shuffle strums which is simply when the strum going down is slower than the strum going up. Like the pattern we looked at before where you miss a strum going up or down, the swing strum is simply a way of making the basic up and down strum a bit catchier.

➢ Another way of making the simple up and down strum a bit more exciting is to hit the palm of your hand on the body in between a beat of strumming up and down to get a drum tap as well.

➢ You can also use your fretting hand – your left hand if you are playing right-handed – to influence your strumming. As you strum, it makes the strings of the ukulele vibrate. To create an impact, use your fret hand to hold down the strings at the top to stop the strings making a sound.

Using a Plectrum

There is a bit of a debate about using a plectrum with the ukulele, although it is generally accepted nowadays to use a pick or plectrum.

The ukulele came from Hawaii when instruments left behind by the Portuguese explorers were modified and adjusted to create something distinctly new. In these days, the Hawaiians didn't use picks, simply relying on their hands – in particular, their index finger and thumb – to strum and create music. As a result, the most popular and regular way of playing the ukulele is just with the fingers.

As the ukulele became known worldwide, some people who were used to playing the guitar or other similar instruments, started playing the ukulele with a pick. Nowadays, it is totally fine to use a pick to play the ukulele and some players like to use a mix of both fingers and a plectrum to create a different sound and produce adapted melodies such as rock music.

Some players though, insist that the ukulele can't be played with a pick due to its traditional roots of being played only with the fingers. If you want to follow the older traditions, then playing with the fingers is fine. If you don't mind embracing the modern influences, use a pick too. Some players don't use a pick but grow their fingernails and use that instead! It's all down to personal preference at the end of the day and there is no right or wrong way.

What Kind of Pick?

The type of pick will depend on a couple of factors, one being the size of your ukulele. Th baritone ukulele, for example, uses a long pick that would be tricky to use with smaller ukuleles. Another point to consider is the material of the strings. If the ukulele has nylon strings, a lighter pick will be perfectly fine. Metal strings may need something a little heavier.

How About Using a Guitar Pick with the Ukulele?

A common question when it comes to picks is whether a guitar pick can be used as a ukulele pick. The answer ultimately boils down to personal opinions – some believe that a guitar pick shouldn't be anywhere near a ukulele – but although the size can be a bit different, some guitar picks are fine to use with a ukulele.

A lot of ukulele picks are made from felt or leather so are kinder on the strings. As a guitar pick tends to be harder, there is the worry that it can harm the ukulele strings. However, a harder pick will not cause significantly different damage and strings will always be exposed to general wear and tear and will need replacing eventually anyway. Using a strong fingernail enthusiastically will cause the same damage as a hard guitar pick. This shouldn't be too much of a concern.

An advantage of using a guitar pick is that its allows you to experiment with different sounds and create unique sounding beats. Don't be afraid to test out a guitar pick. You never know, if you really like the sound of it, it can encourage you to produce some fantastic music that is quite unique from anything else!

Will a Pick Damage Your Ukulele?

Not really. If you attack your strings with over-enthusiasm on the pick then you may quicken the rate of general wear and tear. But strings are not built or made for life and eventually you will have to replace them at some point. Using a pick won't have a significant effect on when you need to buy a new set of strings.

So, What's the Conclusion? To Use a Pick or Not?

It's totally up to you. It's worth experimenting with both fingers only and testing out a pick to get an idea for the different sounds. Always remember that you are the musician and you produce your own music so whatever you feel sounds the best, you should stick to. There is no right or wrong way which is why music is so creative.

Overall, a harder pick will help add a bit more volume to your music and protect your fingers a bit. This is especially true if you like playing faster beats. Use a leather or felt pick if you want a softer sound that doesn't produce an after 'clicking' sound that harder picks sometimes make.

As picks generally aren't that expensive, you can buy a few and see which ones you like the most. As you get more experienced, you may find that you lean towards certain picks automatically depending on the sound you want to produce and the music that you are playing.

Chapter Summary

In this chapter, we looked at everything you need to know about strumming.

- The basic technique of strumming is to simply flick the wrist to move the hand up and down over the strings that lie across the sound hole.

- The best place to strum largely depends on your ukulele but generally, the best sound is produced near to where the neck and the body meet.

- You can jazz up basic strumming by missing a strum, using the body to make a percussion sound, or holding the strings on the neck with your fretting hand to get a crisp finish.

- You can use a pick or plectrum if you like. It usually comes down to personal preference.

In the next chapter, we will look at reading tabs.

Chapter Six: Lesson Five: How to Read Tabs

In this chapter, we will look at how to read tabs, an essential skill in learning the ukulele.

The first question is – what is a tab and why do you need to read it?

It's a good question.

A tab is another way of saying music tablature, which is basically a sheet of paper that represents the music that you need to play. It is commonly used among the stringed instruments, such as the ukulele.

The main advantage of a tab is that it isn't that hard to read. It may seem strange in the beginning but it's easy to pick up, especially with practice. It is certainly possible to understand some key parts in one day so that you can start playing some songs on the ukulele almost straight away.

If you have never had formal music training, don't fret. The tab doesn't require it at all. It tells you exactly which string to use to play a certain note and where to play that note on the fretboard. It really makes life easy when it comes to following a particular song.

We will start by reading notes in a tab before later moving onto chords in a tab.

The best way of learning is to see some examples.

```
A ------------------------------------------
E ------------------------------------------
C ------------------------------------------
G ------------------------------------------
```

This is the general tab table with each horizontal line representing the string of the ukulele and it is labelled accordingly. You may have expected the tab to be the other way around with the top line starting as the G string as when you are playing, the A string is the one that is closest to your body or the floor. If you imagine the head of the ukulele being on the left-hand side of this tab, it can help get some perspective on that.

You will notice on the tab that there are numbers placed on the different strings (or horizontal lines, literally speaking).

```
        A-----2------------------------------
E----------0----------------------0-----
C----------------0----------0----------
G--------------------0----------------
```

The above is purely an example. The number on each string shows which fret number you need to play. So, the above shows we would play the A string on the third fret, then an open E string, then the open C string, then down to the open G string and continue like that.

If that's a bit confusing, let's look at this in more details, in particular, for open notes.

Here is another example.

```
      A-----------------------------------
E------1----------------------------
C-----------------------------------
G-----------------------------------
```

Here, we can see that there is a '1' on the E string. This means that you need to just play this string on the first fret. So, you would hold the E string on the first fret and pluck that with your finger.

Then, we have this example.

```
      A-----------------------------------
E------0----------------------------
C-----------------------------------
G-----------------------------------
```

To play this, we would play the E string without fretting. In other words, we would pluck the E string without holding it down.

That is how to play the chords when the numbers are scattered across the tab like we saw above – you pluck the strings. Let's look at something a little different now.

Chords in a Tab

Whereas above we saw how to pluck certain strings, we will now see how to read chords presented on the strings.

Let's take a look at the following:

```
    A--------0-----------
E--------1-----------
C-------0-----------
G-------2-----------
```

As you can see, we have a vertical line of numbers. This represents a chord. So, you would hold down the E string on the first fret and the G string on the second fret. You would leave the other strings untouched and then strum the strings across the sound hole.

This would give you the F chord.

Let's look at another example, but this time a sequence of chords.

```
    A-----2-----3-----0-----0-----3-----2-----
E-----3-----0-----0-----1-----2-----1-----
C-----2-----0-----0-----0-----2-----2-----
G-----0-----0-----2-----2-----2-----0-----
```

This tab shows several chords in a row. In this sequence, we can see that the chords to play are G then C then Am then F then D7 and finally, G7.

This is a really easy way of reading chords and it helps if the chords are written above the vertical lines, as they often are.

The only downside of this style of reading chords is that it is tricky to work out the beat and pace of the song if you don't already know it. The key then is to listen to the song before and get a feel for the beat. Then you can play the chords accordingly.

Sometimes, you may see arrows next to the chords that point up or down. These arrows may be straight or wavy, but they mean the same thing. The arrows simply indicate which way you should strum and it works in a logical order. The arrow pointing up means you should strum up and the arrow pointing down means – you got it – you should strum down.

If you understood all of that, then you are already perfectly capable of reading notes and chords at a great level!

What we will look at now are a couple of slightly more advanced moves. To get the basics of the ukulele in one day, you may not need to utilize the following two concepts immediately, but it's worth knowing what 'hammer-ons' and 'pull-offs' are anyway.

Hammer-Ons

When you come across a tab that looks like this below, it is known as a hammer-on note.

```
     A-----1-------------------
E-----1-------------------
C-----------1h2----------
G------------------2-----
```

You can notice the 'h' in between the two notes on the third line. This 'h' represents the 'hammer on'. A hammer on is basically when you pluck a note on the ukulele string and then place a finger on a higher fret to produce a higher-sounding note.

You may see the hammer-on being represented by an arch between the notes, but here we see it as a 'h'. In the above example, the C string is played on the first fret and then your other finger will quickly hold down (hammer-on) the second fret to produce two notes while the string is plucked just once.

The next concept is pull-offs.

Pull Offs

Pull offs are the perfect opposite of hammer-ons. This time, you play a note and produce a second note that is lower than the first one. It can either be represented by a 'p' or by arches in between the two notes. When you see arches on a tab, the way to distinguish whether it is a hammer-on or a pull-off is the sequence of numbers. A pull-off will show numbers that go from higher to lower and a hammer-on will show numbers going from lower to higher.

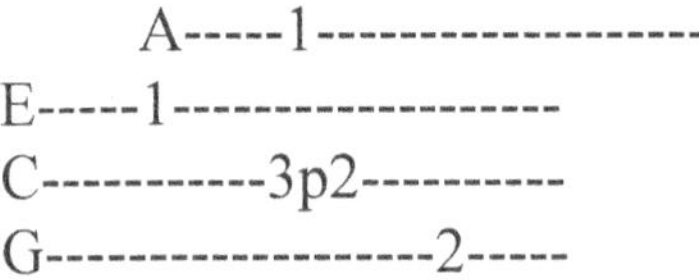

Here we can see the pull off is on the third line – the C string. What we would do here is play the C string on the third fret and pull off – or hold down – the same string but on the second fret to produce a note without plucking the string again.

Chapter Summary

In this chapter, we learned about how to read tabs. This is important to be able to play songs and music on the ukulele.

• We first looked at how to play notes where you would pluck the strings rather than strum. The tabs show you which note to play and which fret to play it in. Sometimes, you will see a '0' which represents an open string. This means you don't hold the string down and instead just pluck it openly.

• We then looked at reading chords on the tabs where the vertical line of numbers shows the strings you need to play and the frets you need to use to form a particular chord. It's an easy way to read chords – so long as you remember how the chords are made! You may want to jot down the chord letters at the top of the tab.

• Finally, we look at two slightly more advanced parts of the tab which are hammer-ons and pull-offs.

In the next chapter, we will look at lesson six which is all about fingerstyle or fingerpicking as it is also known as.

Chapter Seven: Lesson Six: Getting the Basics of Fingerstyle

In this chapter, we will look at fingerstyle.

First, what is fingerstyle?

Fingerstyle is a style of playing the ukulele with just your fingers and is known as finger picking. If you are used to strumming, especially guitar players, you may find this a bit unnatural in the beginning but as with anything, with practice, it becomes second nature eventually.

There are two ways to fingerpick when playing the ukulele. There may be variations on these, but these are the two most popular and common ways.

➢ One way is to use your thumb, index finger, and your middle finger together. You thumb is in charge of plucking the top two strings – so G and C – then your index finger plucks the next string – the E string – and finally, your middle finger is responsible for plucking the A string.

➢ The other way uses an extra finger – the ring finger. So, your thumb plucks the G string, your index plucks the C string, then your middle finger does the E string and your ring finger plucks the A string.

Which one is the best? Neither is better than the other, it depends on what you feel the most comfortable with. You may actually find yourself using both techniques as you become more advanced, especially as some music patterns you may find easier when you use more fingers. Try practicing with styles to get a feel for which one you like the most.

For the sake of keeping things easy, we will stick to the first technique here and just use three fingers.

Let's begin our practise.

Take a look at the tab below.

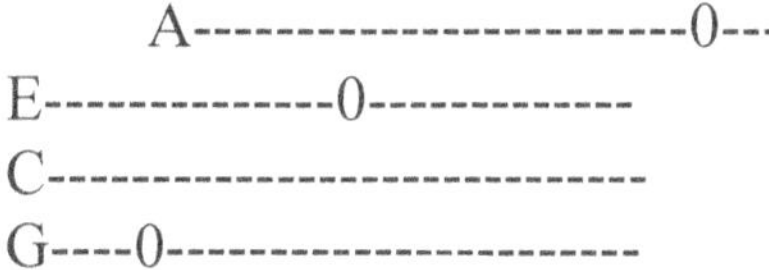

Here, this tab gives you the opportunity to use all fingers required. The G you play with your thumb – the C string you play with your thumb too but in this case, we will skip the C – then the E string you play with your index finger and finally, the A string you play with your middle finger.

Don't worry about the left, fretting hand for now. Simply focus on the right hand and pluck these notes above the sound hole. So, pluck the G first with the thumb, then pluck the E next with the index finger, and then pluck the A to finish with your middle finger.

Keep doing the same sequence several times until you get the rhythm.

At the moment, you are just playing notes and you get that nice, unfinished sound when you pluck the strings. Next, we will add a chord in the mix. Now you must use your left hand to make the chord and your right hand will pluck the strings. It's interesting to hear how the open string makes a different sound to the chord which sounds more closed and tinny when it's played.

Let's look at the following.

```
A-------------------------3--------
E---------------0-----------------
C--------------------------------
G-------0------------------------
```

Here, we've added in the C chord which you play on the A string on the third fret. So, make the C chord with your left hand. Now, pluck the open G string with your thumb, then the open E string with your index finger, and finally, pluck the A string as it is formed in the C chord.

Keep repeating that pattern to get used to the feel.

Let's add in an A chord now.

```
A------------------------0---------
E--------------------------------
C--------------1-----------------
G-------2------------------------
```

Here, you make the A chord with your left hand by holding the G string on the second fret and the C string on the first fret. Then, you pluck the G string with you thumb, the C string with your thumb again and then pluck the A string on an open string with your middle finger.

Try alternating between the two chords. Play the C chord a couple of times with the open G and E string then play the A chord a couple of times with the open A string to really practice your fingerpicking.

Another easy chord is the F chord. Try fingerpicking several chords instead of strumming to get used to this style of playing.

Here is a short pattern to help you practice. Keep playing this pattern on repeat until you feel you're getting the hang of fingerpicking. A good tip is to keep your hand rested on the body of the ukulele to help keep it steady.

```
A-------3--------------2-------------0---------------2-------
E-----0-----0------3------3-----1-------1--------3------3---
C--0-----------2--------------0------------2--------------
G-----------------------------------------------------------
```

Play this slowly and then challenge yourself to try playing it faster. Remember not to strum but to pluck each string.

Chapter Summary

In this chapter, we looked at the art of fingerstyle to play the ukulele.

- Fingerstyle is a way of playing the ukulele. It depends on plucking the stings to play certain notes or chords rather than strumming.

• Start by practicing fingerpicking notes rather than chords. It will help get you used to using you thumb, index finger, and middle finger for playing.

• Once you are comfortable with fingerpicking notes, move onto chords and keep practicing sequences of chords to get used to it.

In the next chapter, we will look at the final lesson which is practicing everything we have learnt and bringing it all together by playing some simple songs.

Chapter Eight: Lesson Seven: Songs to Play

In this chapter, we will look at some simple songs that you can now play on your ukulele.

Over the last six lessons, you have learnt everything you need to know to play the ukulele in one day. You have learnt all about the chords, how to strum, how to fingerpick, how to read notes, and how to read chords. Now, in the final lesson, we will bring all that together for the grand finale – playing songs with the ukulele. This is probably one of the most satisfying parts of the ukulele, coming second only to creating your own music.

Here are some songs for you to play with the chords and the lyrics. You should recognise some but if not, simply search for them online to find out the tune and play along to the rhythm.

How about we start with a Beatles classic? It may seem a bit complicated but it's actually pretty easy to play. You will feel great after playing this after just one day of learning the ukulele!

The Beatles – Let it Be

For this song you need to know four chords – C, G Am, and
F

The intro starts with: C – G – Am – F – C – G – F – C

Verse

      C   G

When I find myself in times of trouble

  Am   F

Mother Mary comes to me

  C   G   F C

Speaking words of wisdom, let it be

   C   G

And in my hour of darkness

    Am   F

She is standing right in front of me

  C   G   F C

Speaking words of wisdom, let it be

Chorus

    Am   G   F   C

Let it be, let it be, let it be, let it be

  Am   G   F C

Whisper words of wisdom, let it be

Verse

    C   G

And when the broken-hearted people

  Am   F

Living in the world agree

  C   G   F

There will be an answer, let it be

  C   G

For though they may be parted

    Am   F

There is still a chance that they will see

  C   G   F C

There will be an answer, let it be

Chorus

    Am   G   F   C

Let it be, let it be, let it be, let it be

```
          Am                    G          F  C
Yeah there will be an answer, let it be
          Am        G       F        C
Let it be, let it be, let it be, let it be
    Am                  G          F   C
Whisper words of wisdom, let it be


F – C – G – F – C – x2
```

Solo

```
C – G – Am – F- C- G - F – C – x2
```

Chorus

```
        Am     G        F        C
Let it be, let it be, let it be, let it be
    Am                  G          F  C
Whisper words of wisdom, let it be
```

Verse

```
        C                  G
And when the night is cloudy
          Am                  F
There is still a light that shines in me
```

| C   G   F C
Shine on until tomorrow, let it be
      C   G
I wake up to the sound of music
     Am   F
Mother Mary comes to me
       C   G   F C
Speaking words of wisdom, let it be

Chorus

       Am   G   F   C
Let it be, let it be, let it be, let it be
         Am   G   F C
Yeah there will be an answer, let it be
        Am   G   F   C
Let it be, let it be, let it be, let it be
       Am   G   F   C
Whisper words of wisdom, let it be

Adele – Someone Like You

The next song is a quite well-known pop song. It's 'Someone Like You' by Adele

Like the Beatles song above, you just need to know G, C, Am, and F chords. Just with four chords, you will be able to play two great songs!

Verse

  C   C

I heard that you're settled down

     Am

That you found a girl

      F

And you're married now

  C   C

I heard that your dreams came true

     Am

Guess she gave you things

     F

I didn't give to you

  C   C

Old friend why are you so shy

     Am

It ain't like you to hold back

  F

Or hide from life

  G   Am   F

I hate to turn up out of the blue uninvited but

     F

I couldn't stay away I couldn't fight it

   G

I'd hoped you'd see my face

  Am   F

And that you'd be reminded that for me it isn't over

Chorus

C   G   Am F

Never mind, I'll find someone like you

   C   G   Am F

I wish nothing but the best for you too

   C   G   Am   F

Don't forget me I beg I re-member you said

     C   G   Am F

Sometimes it lasts in love but sometimes it hurts in-stead

     C   G   Am F

Sometimes it lasts in love but sometimes it hurts instead, yeah

Verse

C   C

You'd know how time flies

  Am

Only yesterday

   F

was the time of our lives

   C

We were born and raised

  C

In a summer haze

  Am   F

Bound by the surprise of our glory days

 G   Am   F

I hate to turn up out of the blue uninvited but

F

I couldn't stay away I couldn't fight it

  G

I'd hoped you'd see my face

  Am   F   F

And that you'd be reminded that for me it isn't over

Chorus

C   G   Am F

Never mind, I'll find someone like you

    C   G   Am F

I wish nothing but the best for you too

    C   G   Am   F

Don't forget me I beg I remember you said

        C   G   Am   F

Sometimes it lasts in love but sometimes it hurts in-stead,
yeah

G

Nothing compares no worries or cares

Am

Regrets and mistakes their memories make

F

 Who would have known how

    Dm   Em   F

Bitter-sweet this would taste

Chorus

C   G   Am F

Never mind I'll find someone like you

241

Never mind I'll find someone like you

```
    C            G      Am F
```
I wish nothing but the best for you too
```
    C        G      Am       F
```
Don't forget me I beg I re-member you said
```
         C            G              Am   F
```
Sometimes it lasts in love but sometimes it hurts in-stead

Chorus

```
C          G              Am F
```
Never mind I'll find someone like you
```
     C         G       Am F
```
I wish nothing but the best for you too
```
    C       G      Am       F
```
Don't forget me I beg I re-member you said
```
         C            G              Am   F
```
Sometimes it lasts in love but sometimes it hurts in-stead
```
         C            G              Am   F
```
Sometimes it lasts in love but sometimes it hurts in-stead
```
         C            G              Am   F
```
Sometimes it lasts in love but sometimes it hurts instead

Leonard Cohen – Hallelujah

This song requires an extra chord compared to the others, so it gives you a bit more of a challenge. For this song, you need to know G, C, F, Am, and Em.

Verse

    C   Am

I've heard there was a secret chord

    C   Am

That David played, and it pleased the Lord

    F   G   C   G

But you don't really care for music, do you?

Chorus

    C   F   G

It goes like this, the fourth and the fifth

    Am   F

The minor fall, the major lift

    G   Em   Am

The baffled king composing hallelujah

Chorus

    F   Am

Hallelujah, hallelujah

    F   C-G-C-C

Hallelujah, hallelujah

Verse

     C   Am

Your faith was strong, but you needed proof

     C   Am

You saw her bathing on the roof

    F   G   C   G

Her beauty in the moonlight overthrew you

    C

She tied you

    F   G

to a kitchen chair

    Am

She broke your throne

    F

She cut your hair

    G   Em   Am

And from your lips she drew the Hallelujah

Chorus

    F   Am

Hallelujah, hallelujah

    F   C-G-C-C

Hallelujah, hallelujah

Verse

 C   Am

Maybe I've been here before

  C   Am

I know this room, I've walked this floor

   F   G   C   G

I used to live alone before I knew you

Pre-chorus

   C   F   G

I've seen your flag on the marble arch

 Am   F

Love is not a victory march

   G   Em   Am

It's a cold and it's a broken hallelujah

Chorus

    F   Am

Hallelujah, hallelujah

      F   C-G-C-C

Hallelujah, hallelujah

Verse

        C   Am

There was a time you'd let me know

   C   Am

What's real and going on below

     F   G   C   G

But now you never show it to me, do you?

Pre-chorus

     C   F   G

Remember when I moved in with you?

   Am   F

The holy dark was moving too

   G   Em   Am

And every breath we drew was hallelujah

Chorus

     F   Am

Hallelujah, hallelujah

     F   C-G-C-C

Hallelujah, hallelujah

Verse

    C   Am
Maybe there's a God above
     C   Am
And all I ever learned from love
       F   G   C   G
Was how to shoot at someone who outdrew you
Pre-chorus
       C   F   G
It's not a cry you can hear at night
    Am   F
It's not somebody who's seen the light
      GE   Em   Am
It's a cold and it's a broken hallelujah

Chorus

   F   Am
Hallelujah, hallelujah
   F   C-G
Hallelujah, hallelujah
   F   Am
Hallelujah, hallelujah

   F   C-G-C

Hallelujah, hallelujah

Chapter Summary

In this chapter, we looked at three songs that will help you learn to play music on the ukulele in one day.

- We looked at three songs – The Beatles, Let it Be; Adele, Someone Like You; and Leonard Cohen, Hallelujah.

- These songs only need knowledge of five chords so if you learn those, you will quickly be playing the ukulele.

Final Words

Congratulations! You have reached the end of 'How to Play Ukulele: In 1 Day - The Only 7 Exercises You Need to Learn Ukulele Chords, Ukulele Tabs and Fingerstyle Ukulele Today.'

By now, you should have a good foundation of knowledge to be able to play the ukulele and even play a couple of songs. You should be able to read chords and know how to both strum and fingerpick to music.

I hope my book has encouraged you to keep learning and building your skills, so you can become a successful and experienced ukulele player. It's a great instrument – have fun playing it!